WITHDRAWN
L. R. COLLEGE LIBRARY

974.02
W73h

67959

DATE DUE			
Dec 5 69			
GAYLORD M-2			PRINTED IN U.S.A.

WITHDRAWN

BURT FRANKLIN: RESEARCH & SOURCE WORKS SERIES 312
American Classics in HIstory & Social Science 60

Hypocrisie Unmasked

by

Edward Winslow

1646

Hypocrisie Unmasked
A True Relation

Of the Proceedings of the
Governor and Company of the *Massachusetts*
Against
Samuel Gorton of *Rhode Island*

By
EDWARD WINSLOW, *Governor*
of the *Plymouth* Colony

Reprinted from the Original Edition
issued at London in 1646
With an Introduction by
HOWARD MILLAR CHAPIN

BURT FRANKLIN
NEW YORK

CARL A. RUDISILL LIBRARY
LENOIR RHYNE COLLEGE

974.02
W 13 L
67959
November, 1969

Published by BURT FRANKLIN
235 East 44th St., New York, N.Y. 10017
Originally Published: 1916
Reprinted: 1968
Printed in the U.S.A.

Library of Congress Catalog Card No.: 68-57130
Burt Franklin: Research and Source Works Series 312
American Classics in History & Social Science 60

Introduction

By

Howard Millar Chapin

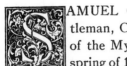AMUEL GORTON, styling himself variously, Gentleman, Citizen of London, Clothier, and Professor of the Mysteries of Christ, landed at Boston in the spring of 1637. He soon settled at Plymouth, where he defied those in authority with vituperative condemnations. His chief complaints were that the magistrates disregarded the common law of England, and administered injustice by means of trials before packed juries which mocked at legal forms. His enthusiasm and his freedom of speech brought him into the power of the magistrates, by whom, on Tuesday, December 4, 1638, he was tried and banished from Plymouth Colony. He departed, with his family, to the newly-settled town of Pocasset upon the island of Aquidneck, now called Portsmouth upon Rhode Island. Here, already, the rivalry and animosity between the factions of William Coddington and of Anne Hutchinson had almost reached the danger-point, and was soon to break forth in an embittered controversy, which under various leaders was to rack and stunt for years the colony about Narragansett Bay.

Gorton joined the liberal Hutchinsonians, who for the nonce obtained the upper hand. By a coup d'état Gorton and Mrs. Hutchinson brought about the election of William Hutchinson, "a man of very mild temper and weak parts, and wholly guided by his wife," as judge in place of Coddington. In describing this conspiracy to his friend, Governor Winthrop, Coddington wrote: "It was hatched when I was last in the Baye, & the Lord, I hope, will shortely putt an esaw to it." Realizing that he was worsted, Coddington and his followers withdrew from Pocasset to the southern end of the island, where they founded Newport. Those who remained at Pocasset changed the name to Portsmouth, and drew up a new Civil Compact. In this document the hand of Gorton is evident, for its signers acknowledged themselves not only subjects of the King, but also obedient to his laws, or in other words subject to the common law of England.

Coddington was elected Governor by the Newport men, and immediately endeavored to extend his authority over the whole island. He had kept possession of the official records, and held in himself the title to the land, which latter advantage largely enabled him to regain the ascendency. Gorton was tried, as at Plymouth, by an indigenous court, which had been sanctioned neither by the King nor by Parliament, and which did not show any particular regard for the forms and practices of English law. Gorton, convinced that the proceedings of the Court were extra-legal, and that he had as much right to try these self-appointed judges as they had to try him, yet feeling powerless against their superior physical force, lost his temper and tersely described various persons present by such expressive terms as "Just Asses," "saucy boys," and "Jack-an-Apes,"; called the Deputy Governor, William Brenton, "an Abetter of Riot, Assault, and Battery," and upon being commanded to prison, imperiously resisted the authority, and made open proclamation, saying, "Take away Coddington, and carry him to prison." Then the Governor said again, "All you that owne the King, take away Gorton and carry him to prison." Gorton replied, "All you that owne the King, take away Coddington, and carry him to prison."

The increase in Coddington's power made Gorton's residence at Portsmouth no longer possible, and in the winter of 1640/41 he removed to Providence. His familistic religious mysticism fascinated many, both at Plymouth and Portsmouth, and six or seven of his disciples with their families accompanied him to Providence.

On March 8, 1640/41, Roger Williams wrote: "Master Gorton having foully abused both high and low at Aquedneck, is now bewiching and bemadding poor Providence." His mysticism and his attacks upon the unchartered government evidently caused a considerable stir in Providence. On May 25, 1641, William Arnold wrote to the board of disposers, who governed Providence, and gave many reasons why the "said Gorton nor his company are not fitt persons to be received in and made members of the town fellowship."

His opposition to the autogenous township inspired his followers to a riot on Monday, November 15, 1641, which led to the formation of three parties at Providence. Gorton and his friends openly defied the unchartered government. Roger Williams, at the head of the law and order party, endeavored to maintain the independent self-government of the town and to conciliate the hostile factions. The third party was led by the ambitious Arnolds, William and his son Benedict, who feared Gorton and were jealous of Williams. This last group of related families had built houses at Pawtuxet, some five miles south of Providence, on the west shore of the Bay. Holding Pawtuxet, they finally seceded from their neighbors and submitted themselves to the jurisdiction of the Massachusetts Bay Colony on September 8, 1642. This union, so clearly hostile to Gorton, led the Gortonoges, as he and his followers were called by the Indians, to move from Providence to the less accessible wilds and marshes of Shawomet, where they purchased land of the sachem Miantonomi, on the 12th of January, 1642/43.

Here, about ten miles south of Providence, on the coves which indent the western shores of Narragansett Bay, Gorton and his followers began to plant and build. The quarrels between the Gortonoges at Shawomet and their neighbors, the Arnolds at Pawtuxet, increased in intensity. The Arnolds complained, as Winslow relates, to their newly-adopted rulers, the magistrates of Massachusetts Bay, who thereupon summoned the Gortonoges to appear at the Boston Court. The latter, claiming subjection only to the English crown, refused to recognize the authority of Massachusetts Bay, and replied with a warrant for the Arnolds to appear for trial at Shawomet. The Massachusetts officials, seeing an opportunity to obtain the much-coveted "outlet into Narragansett Bay," forthwith sent an expeditionary army of forty men against Shawomet in

September, 1643. A battle ensued in which the Massachusetts
Bay soldiery shot to pieces the English flag, which Gorton had
raised upon his house. Happily, no one was killed. After
a siege of several days the opposing commanders suspended
hostilities and met in conference. By violating this truce, the
Massachusetts' commander, Captain George Cooke, captured
Gorton and his chief men, and then led them in a triumphal
procession through Providence to Boston, where they were
sentenced "to work for their living, and wear irons upon one
leg and not to depart the limits of the town," during the pleasure
of the court. Their property was confiscated to pay the expenses
of the expedition, while their religious views were used to salve
the consciences of the members of the court. Their families,
left destitute, fled for refuge to Providence and Portsmouth.

Finding that Gorton and his company spread heretical doctrines where they were confined, the court, "not knowing what
to do with them, at length agreed to set them at liberty" in
March, 1644. Upon regaining their freedom, the Gortonoges
returned to Portsmouth, and appointed commissioners, who
joined with those of the other towns in acting under the recently-
received Charter of 1643. Coddington refused to recognize
this Charter, which Roger Williams had secured by personal
application in London, and with his faction endeavored to
"maintain the government as before," as he wrote to Winthrop
in 1646. He continued his intrigues with Massachusetts Bay
and Plymouth, until his usurpation of power in 1651.

On Friday, April 19, 1644, soon after his release by Massachusetts Bay, Gorton obtained from the Narragansett sachems
an act of submission and allegiance to the English crown.
Armed with this and a fluent pen, he sailed for England in the
autumn of 1645. Upon arriving in London, Gorton, on behalf
of himself and his friends, petitioned the King and Parliament
for redress and for reinstatement at Shawomet. He also published, in 1646, as a part of his campaign against his enemies:
"Simplicities Defence against Seven-Headed Policy. Or a true

complaint of a peaceable people, being part of the English in New England, made unto the state of Old England, against cruell persecutors United in Church-Government;" a narrative of 111 closely printed pages recounting the unlawful and wicked actions of Massachusetts Bay in persecuting him and his followers.

The leaders of Massachusetts Bay and Plymouth, fearing the effect of Gorton's pen and tongue, commissioned Edward Winslow on December 4, 1646, to hasten to England and use his influence to counteract the work of the troublesome Gorton, and to further the ambitious territorial designs of these two colonies. As Governor Winthrop wrote: "Mr. Winslow's instructions were of two sorts; the one (which he might publish, etc. . . . The other were more secret, . . . "

The envoy, whom Roger Williams describes as "That great and pious soul, Mr. Winslow," was the scion of a landed family of Worcestershire. He was born at Droitwich, on Saturday, October 18, 1595. He traveled on the continent, when a young man, and became acquainted with the Rev. John Robinson in Holland. In 1617 he joined the separatist church at Leyden, and on May 16, 1618, was married there to Elizabeth Barker. The twenty-fifth anniversary of his birthday he celebrated, or at least passed, on board the *Mayflower*, during her famous voyage. His wife died March 29, 1620/21, and within two months he was married again, on May 12th, to the widow, Susanna White, whose six-months-old son, Peregrine, was the first English child born in New England.

Winslow took a leading part in the negotiations with Ousamequin, alias Massasoit, which resulted in the understanding between the Wampanoags and Plymouth. He explored Boston Harbor, traded with the Dutch, and remained on terms of the closest friendship with Massasoit. In 1623, he returned to England with Robert Cushman, as agent for the Colony, and in the next year issued his "Good Newes from New England: or A true Relation of things very remarkable at the Plantation of

Plimoth in NEW-ENGLAND. Shewing the wondrous providence
and goodness of GOD, in their preservation and continuance,
being delivered from many apparant deaths and dangers." He
returned to Plymouth in the spring of 1624, but in the sum-
mer again went to England on behalf of the Colony.   In this
year, 1624, he was elected a member of the Court of Assistants,
the governing board of the Colony, which office he held, except
when he was Governor, until his departure for England in 1646.

   In 1633, Winslow was elected Governor of the Colony.   He
had from the first been the leader in managing the commercial
affairs of this Colony, which was a business venture as well as a
religious settlement, with financial backers who expected mone-
tary returns.   During the following year, when returning from a
trading expedition, he stopped at Sowams to visit his old friend
Massasoit.   The humorous Indian sent a messenger to Plymouth announcing the sad tidings of Winslow's death, thus
throwing the Colonists into mourning and lamentations.   The
next morning Massasoit, accompanied by Winslow himself,
arrived at Plymouth to the stupefaction and delight of the
Colonists.   The Sachem explained that he had sent the false
message in order to make their arrival more welcome.

   In 1635, he again visited England on a diplomatic mission
for Massachusetts Bay and Plymouth.   He was accused by
Archbishop Laud, a political opponent, of having solemnized
marriages, although a layman, and upon being convicted of
this, he was committed to the Fleet prison and kept there for
seventeen weeks.   After his return to Plymouth, he was again
chosen Governor, in 1636.   In 1643, Winslow represented
Plymouth at the meetings of the Confederation of the United
Colonies of New England; in 1644, was again chosen Governor;
and in 1645 he was President of the Council of War at Plymouth.

   In December, 1646, he was sent to England once more, this
time to oppose the efforts of Samuel Gorton and of the Hingham
petitioners, who from within, as Gorton from without, were
agitating the question of the repeated violation of English law

by the theocratic despots of Boston. Winthrop described Winslow at this time as "a fit man to be employed in our affairs in England, both in regard to his abilities of presence, speech, courage and understanding, as also being well known to the commissioners," who directed colonial affairs at this time.

Upon reaching England, Winslow was confronted with Gorton's book describing the wickedness of the theocratic politicians of Plymouth and the Bay, and so in an unsuccessful attempt to discredit Gorton and his book, immediately wrote and issued "Hypocrisie Unmasked By a true Relation of the Proceedings of the Governour and Company of the Massachusets against Samuel Gorton (and his Accomplices) a notorious disturber of the Peace and quiet of the severall Governments wherein he lived . . . " It is this work which, in the following pages, is printed for the first time in America.

A manuscript copy of what appears to have been a variant of part of Winslow's original draft was printed in the New England Historical and Genealogical Register for 1850, with notes by Charles Deane.

A portion of Winslow's tract, that which deals with "the true grounds or cause of the first planting of New England," was printed by Alexander Young, in his "Chronicles of the Pilgrim Fathers," in 1841, pp. 379-408.

The complete text of each of the other tracts of this controversial series is accessible in nineteenth-century editions. Gorton's "Simplicities Defence" forms the second volume of the Rhode Island Historical Society's Collections, Providence, 1835, with notes by William R. Staples. It was printed again at Washington, D. C., in 1846, as No. 6 in the fourth volume of Peter Force's "Tracts."

Child's "New England's Jonas" was reprinted in 1816 in Vol. IV of the second series of the Collections of the Massachusetts Historical Society, pp. 107-120. It also made No. 3 in the fourth volume of Force's Tracts, Washington, 1846.

It was again reprinted, with an introduction by W. T. R. Marvin, by Wm. Parsons Lunt, at Boston in 1869.

Winslow's reply to Child, "New-England's Salamander," was reprinted at Boston in 1830 in Vol. II of the third series of the Massachusetts Historical Society's Collections, pp. 110-145.

"Hypocrisie Unmasked" was reissued in England in 1649, the dedication being omitted and replaced by a table of contents, and the title being changed to "The Danger of tolerating Levellers in a Civill State; or an Historicall Narration of the dangerous, pernicious practices and opinions, wherewith Samuel Gorton and his levelling accomplices so much disturbed and molested the several Plantations in New England . . . " The body of the book is made up of the same sheets as those which had appeared with the original title-page. The omission of the dedication to the Earl of Warwick was doubtless due to the fact that by that time Warwick had shown himself opposed to Winslow's petition, and the change in the title seems to have been made in order to lift the book from the sphere of local political interest to the then broader field of theological discussion, and so enable the bookseller to dispose of the copies remaining on his shelves.

In refuting the more serious of Gorton's charges, Winslow admits many which he considered of less importance, and so inadvertently gives a not very pleasing picture of New England's more powerful colonies.

The present reprint has been made from the copy of "Hypocrisie Unmasked" which is preserved at the *Library of Congress.* The copy of "The Danger of Tolerating Levellers," which is preserved in the Lenox Collection of the *New York Public Library,* has been followed for the table of contents. The title pages are reproduced from the copies at the *Boston Public Library.*

The Reprint

——

The title-page, *The Danger of Tolerating Levellers*, and the two pages of *Contents* are from the reissue of 1649, in which they replace the title-page and dedication of 1646.

Hypocrisie Unmasked

BY

A true Relation of the Proceedings of the Governour and Company of the *Maſſachuſets* againſt SAMVEL GORTON (and his Accomplices) a notorious diſturber of the Peace and quiet of the ſeverall Governments wherein he lived: With the grounds and reaſons thereof, examined and allowed by their Generall Court holden at *Boſton* in *New-England* in *November* laſt, 1646.

Together with a particular Anſwer to the manifold ſlanders, and abominable falſhoods which are contained in a Book written by the ſaid *GORTON*, and entituled, *Simplicities defence againſt Seven-headed Policy, &c.*

DISCOVERING

To the view of all whoſe eyes are open, his manifold Blaſphemies; As alſo the dangerous agreement which he and his Accomplices made with ambitious and treacherous *Indians*, who at the ſame time were deeply engaged in a deſperate Conſpiracy to cut off all the reſt of the *Engliſh* in the other Plantations.

VVhereunto is added a briefe Narration (occaſioned by certain aſperſions) of the true grounds or cauſe of the firſt Planting of *New-England*; the Preſident of their Churches in the way and Worſhip of God; their Communion with the *Reformed Churches*; and their practiſe towards thoſe that diſſent from them in matters of Religion and Church-Government.

By *Edw. Winſlow.*

Pſal. 120.3. *What ſhall be given unto thee, or what ſhall be done unto thee thou falſe tongue?*
Verſ. 4. *Sharpe arrows of the Mighty, with coales of Juniper.*

Publiſhed by Authority.

London, Printed by *Rich. Cotes* for *John Bellamy* at the three Golden Lions in *Cornhill*, neare the Royall Exchange, 1646.

THE
Danger of Tolerating
LEVELLERS
In a Civill State:

OR,

An Historicall Narration of the dangerous pernicious practices and opinions, wherewith *SAMUEL GORTON* and his
Levelling Accomplices so much disturbed and molested the severall Plantations in *NEW-ENGLANE*;
(Parallel to the positions and proceedings of the present
Levellers in *OLD-ENGLAND.*)
Wherein their severall Errors dangerous and
very destructive to the peace both of Church and State,
their cariage and reviling language against Magistracy
and all Civill power, and their blasphemous speeches
against the holy things of God:
TOGETHER,
With the Course that was there taken for suppressing them,
are fully sot forth;
With a Satisfactory Answer to their Complaints made
to the PARLIAMENT:

By *Edw. Winslow* of *Plymouth* in *New-England.*

London, Printed by *Rich. Cotes* for *John Bellamy* at the three Golden
Lions in *Corn-hill,* neare the Royall Exchange, 1649.

The Contents.

The

The Contents.

TO THE
RIGHT HONOVRABLE
ROBERT

Earl of *Warwick*, Governour in Chiefe,
and Lord High Admirall of all thofe Iflands and
other Plantations of the *Englifh* in AMERICA;
Together with the reft of thofe truly Honorable
Members of both Houfes of Parliament joyned in
Commiffion with him for ordering the
affaires of the faid *Plantations*.

Right Honourable,

 *Ere not your Wifdome and experience in the
great and weighty affaires of State fo well
known, and were yee not fo much accuftomed
to the unjuft complaints of clamorous perfons,
I might be difcouraged to appeare in the righteous caufe of the* United Colonies of New-
England, *and more efpecially in the behalf of the* Governour
and Company of the Maffachufets, *to render a reafon of
their juft and righteous proceedings againft* Samuel Gorton
*and his Companions, who however (where they are unknown)
they goe here under the garbe of a peaceable people; yet if your
Honours, and the reft of the Honourable Committee fhall be
pleafed (when more weighty employments fhall give way) to pe-
rufe our juft defence againft his clamorous complaints, and
fcandalous Treatife, called,* Simplicities defence againft
Seven-

The Epiſtle Dedicatory.

Seven-headed Policy, &c. *I make no queſtion but yee will receive full ſatisfaction in what we have done, and be ready to juſtifie our proceedings againſt them as godly, and righteous.*

The reaſon wherefore I am forced to appeare in Print before I give a particular anſwer to your Honours, and the reſt of the Honourable Committee, is, becauſe I find a more groſſe deformatory aſperſion caſt upon the Countrey to the publick view of our Nation: which as it is deare in our eyes (witneſſe our frequent publick ſolemn dayes of prayer to the Throne of grace for it, together with our private ſupplications, which the Searcher of the heart beſt knows, ſympathizing with it in every condition, to the loſſe of Ships, Goods, &c. to the great weakening of our eſtates) ſo wee deſire to remove whatſoever may ſadden the thoughts of our Nation againſt us; eſpecially your Honours, and all that are godly in Chriſt Jeſus.

What greater wrong can bee done a poore perſecuted people that went into the wilderneſſe to avoid the tyrannicall Government of the late Hierarchy, and to enjoy the Liberties Chriſt Jeſus hath left unto his Churches (which theſe blaſphemous Adverſaries of ours, ſo much ſleight and caſt off) then to be accounted perſecutors of Chriſt in his Saints, yea, to go thither to that end, to become outragiouſly cruell, barbarouſly inhumane, uniting together to ſuck the blood of our Country-men, &c. *And yet Right Honorable, it will and doth appeare in the following Treatiſe, that* Samuel Gorton *was proſecuted againſt, Firſt, at* Plymouth *as a groſſe diſturber of the Civill peace and quiet of that Government, in an open factious and ſeditious manner. Secondly, hee was no leſſe troubleſome, but much more at* Roade Iſland, *having gotten a ſtrong party to adhere unto him, affronting that Government (as* Plymouth) *in their publique adminiſtration of Juſtice ſo foully and groſſely, as mine eares never heard the like of any; to which Relation in the following Diſcourſe I referre*

referre your Honours, being compiled as briefly as may bee.
Gorton *being there whipt in his perſon, and thence baniſhed
with some of his principall adherents, they went next to*
Providence, *where* Mr. Williams, *and ſome others have
built a ſmall Towne. This people receiving them with all
humanity in a cold ſeaſon, when the former places could no
longer beare his inſolencies; hee ſoone undermined their Government, gained a ſtrong party amongſt them to his owne,
to the great diſtraction of* Mr. Williams, *and the better
party there, contending againſt their Laws, and the execution
of Juſtice, to the effuſion of bloud, which made* Mr. Williams *and the reſt ſadly complaine to the Government of the*
Maſſachuſets, *and divers of them take the protection of that
Government, to defend their perſons and eſtates. But when
they ſaw* Mr. Williams *reſolve rather to loſe the benefit of
his labours, then to live with ſuch ill-affected people, and
the neighbour Governments become affected with* Gortons
*miſ-rule there alſo, hee (and his Companions in evill)
began then to thinke of buying a place of a great aſpiring*
Sachim, *or* Indian Prince, *to the wrong of the proper Owners, (two inferiour* Sachims *) who alſo, as well as divers*
Engliſh *of* Providence, *ſubmitted their perſons and lands
to the Government of the* Maſſachuſets, *and deſired their
protection not onely againſt the oppreſſing tyranny of* Myantonimo *the foreſaid Great* Sachim, *but againſt* Gorton *and
his Companions, who intruded into their proper right, by
unwarrantable meanes, &c. Now the Government of the*
Maſſachuſets *having uſed all due meanes and none prevailing, but their gentleneſſe anſwered with the greateſt
contempt that might bee: At the next Meeting of the
Commiſſioners for the United Colonies they complained of* Gorton *and his irregular Companions, which the ſaid Commiſſioners tooke into ſerious conſideration, and the more becauſe*

of

of Gortons, *&c. extraordinary familiarity with* Myantonimo, *and the reſt of the* Nanohigganſet Sachims, *who
were knowne to bee in a deepe Conſpiracy againſt all the Engliſh in the Land at the ſame time. And therefore by a
ſolemne Act gave liberty to the Government of the* Maſſachuſets *to call them to account, and proceed with them ſo
farre as might ſtand with righteouſneſſe and juſtice, which
they accordingly did.*

*Now theſe Right Honourable, &c. are the true cauſes of all
the Cenſures and puniſhments that befell* Gorton *in the
Countrey; onely needleſly in his and their contemptuous anſwers to the modeſt and well-ordered Writingsof the ſaid Government of the* Maſſachuſets, *they belched forth ſuch horrid blaſphemies, not onely againſt them in particular, and
Civill Government in the generall, but againſt the received Chriſtian Religion of all the Reformed Churches in* Eu-
rope, *as well as our ſelves; Inſomuch as many tender Conſciences, both Miniſters and others, thought the Government did not well in giving him ſuch liberty, whereby hee
may and doth (as is reported) poyſon other perſons and
places with his corrupt opinions, to the great diſhonour of
God, and ruine of the ſoules of his followers, who reject the
meanes of grace God hath ſanctified to ſtrenghthen and build up
his people in faith and holineſſe.*

*But that I may not bee tedious, I ſhall preſume to pre-
ferre theſe following requeſts to your Honours and the reſt
of the honoured Committee this Renowned* Parliament *hath
betruſted with the affaires of the Forraigne Plantations of
our Nation: The firſt is to ſtrengthen the Cenſure of the*
Maſſachuſets *by your favourable approbation, ſo farre as it
ſhall appeare to bee juſt and righteous; and then ſhall the
Countrey bee the more preſerved from their feares of the*
Gortonians *deſperate cloſe with ſo dangerous enemies as their*
malig-

malignant neighbours the Nanohigganfets; *which I perfwade my felfe, if your leifures will fuffer you to read the following Difcourfe, you will eafily condefcend unto; there being nothing (I thanke God in it) affirmed by mee, but as it is affirmed hereunto I may fafely depofe. A fecond thing is, that yee will never fuffer* Samuel Gorton *this peftilent difturber of our Societies, any more to goe to* New-England *to difquiet the peace thereof. My third requeft is , that yee will be pleafed to fuffer* New-Plymouth, *to enjoy their former liberty in the line of their Government, which includeth their very feat, even* Shawamet *it felfe, where* Gorton *and his Company dwelt. My fourth requeft is, to take into your ferious confideration , how deftructive it will prove to the well-being of our Plantations and proceedings there, (who by Gods blef-fing are growing up into a Nation) here to anfwer to the com-plaints of fuch malignant fpirits as fhall there bee cenfured by Authority, It being three thoufand miles diftant, fo far as will undoe any to come for Juftice, utterly difabling them to prove the equity of their caufe, unleffe their eftate bee very great. My fifth and laft requeft is, that your Honours , and the reft of the Honoured Committee will be pleafed to patronize the weake labours of your humble fervant , in the juft defence hee hath made for* New-England , *and the feverall Govern-ments of it (efpecially the* Maffachufets) *againft the groffe calumnies of the fore-mentioned fcandalous Treatife publifhed by the faid* Gorton : *And herein yee fhall not onely oblige our Plantations of* New-England *to continue their daily re-queft to the God of all mercies for a bleffing upon this Renow-ned Parliament,and your Honours, and the reft of this Honoured Committee in efpeciall, but to engage with, and for them and you, againft all oppofers of the State, to the laft drop of bloud in our veines; yea, hereby fhall you fweeten the tedious travels, great charges and labours of me their unworthy Agent, who doe*

and

The Epiſtle DEDICATORY.

and ſhall daily pray to God to recompenſe your vaſt hazzards, expenſes, ſtudies, and cares, (to advance the Weale Publike of this diſtreſſed Kingdome, and the ſeverall limbs thereof) with all the bleſſings of Heaven and earth to you and yours to ſucceeding Generations.

Yours Honours humble devoted ſervant,

E DVV. W INSLOVV.

A
TRVE RELATION
OF THE
Proceedings of the Governour and Company of the *Maſſachuſets* in *New-England*, againſt *Samuel Gorton* and his Accomplices; with the grounds and reaſons thereof, examined and allowed by their Generall Court holden at *Boſton* in *November*, 1646.

AMUEL GORTON lived ſometime at *Plymouth*, where his behaviour was ſo turbulent and offenſive both to the Magiſtrates and others, as they were neceſſitated to drive him out of their Juriſdiction. From thence hee went to *Roade-Iſland*, where hee began to raiſe ſedition, and to make a party againſt the Authority there; for which hee was apprehended and whipped, and ſo ſent away. From thence (with ſome others whom hee had gathered to his part) hee removed to *Providence*, where Mr. *Roger Williams* then lived. Hee (with ſome others) oppoſed his ſitting down there as an Inhabitant, onely in regard of his preſent diſtreſſe, they gave way for his abode for a time. But being once houſed, hee ſoon drew ſo great a party to him, as it was beyond the power of Mr. *Williams* and his party to drive them out, or to rule them there; ſo as both parties came armed into the field each againſt other, and had fought it out, had not Mr. *Williams* uſed meanes for pacification.

Hereupon

Hereupon many of the chiefe of *Providence* fent meffengers with a Letter to the Governour and Councell of the *Maffachufets*, defiring aide againft *Gorton* and his company; but they were anfwered, that not being within our Jurifdiction nor confederation we had no ground to interpofe in their quarrells. Soone after fome of thofe men tendred themfelves and their lands to come under our Government, and were received.

There live neere to *Providence* two fmall Indian *Sachims* called *Pumham* and *Socononoco*, who though they are as free as the great *Sachim* of the *Nanohigganfet*: Yet *Myantonimo* the then *Sachim* of of *Nanohigganfet*(being a very proud and fterne man) kept them in great awe. This poore *Sachim Pumham* had a large parcell of land neer *Providence*, very convenient for plantation, which *Gorton* and his company (being now about 13, or 14.) taking notice of, and fearing they fhould not be able to keep their power long where they were, dealt with *Myantonimo* for this parcell of land, promifing him a good parcell of *Wampam* for it. And becaufe they knew that *Pumham* was the true owner of it, they dealt with him alfo; but he refufing to fell it (for hee dwelt upon it, or very neare to it) they caufed *Myantonimo* to fend for him, and having drawn a Writing purporting the fale thereof for a certaine confideration to bee given to both of them, *Myantonimo* figned it, and hee for feare of *Myantonimo* fet his mark to it alfo, not knowing what it was. But when *Gorton* tendred him the confideration for it, hee utterly refufed it, it being the Indians manner not to account any thing fold, till the party have received the thing it is fold for.

But upon this colourable title *Gorton* and his company enter upon the land, and build fome houfes, and withall much wrong the Indians with their cattle, and having *Myantonimo* their friend, behave themfelves very infolently toward the poor Indians, who (having no friends or meanes to relieve themfelves) came and tendred themfelves and their lands to the government of the *Maffachufets*, who (by order of the Court)gave notice thereof to *Myantonimo*, and appointed him to come or fend to the next Court at *Bofton*, to fhew his title or intereft (if hee had any) to the faid *Pumham* and *Socononoco* or their lands. At the time appointed hee came, and pretended that they were his vaffalls, but it appeared clearly both by a writing from Mr. *Williams*, and the teftimony of fome other Englifh in thofe parts, and of divers other Indians no way related to
them,

them, that they were free *Sachims*; ſo as *Myantonimo* having nothing to reply,the Court received the two Indian *Sachims* with their
ſubjects and lands under the government and protection of the
Maſſachuſetts; and upon that writ to our neighbours of *Providence*,
intimating the ſame to them, and adviſing *Gorton* and his company,
that if they had any juſt title to the lands they poſſeſſed,they ſhould
come, or ſend ſome for them to ſhew the ſame to the Court, and
offered them ſafe conduct.   This letter from the Court they tooke
in great diſdaine, and returned ſcornfull and menacing anſwers by
word of mouth, and a good time after they wrote a letter to the
Court full of reproach and blaſphemies,not onely againſt the Magiſtrates,but againſt the Churches and Ordinances, as by the Copy
thereof hereafter following will appeare.   Notwithſtanding theſe
provocations and daily wrongs offered to thoſe few Engliſh their
neighbours (who had formerly ſubmitted themſelves to our Government) wee ſate ſtill neare halfe a yeare, and before we attem-
pted any thing againſt them,wee adviſed with the Commiſſioners of
the united Colonies , who (upon teſtimony of their inſolent and
injurious courſes, and peruſall of the letter they ſent to us)left them
to us to proceed according to Juſtice.   Whereupon the Court ſent
againe to them by two of their members, who carryed letters (to
require and perſwade them to come and give ſatisfaction,)and a ſafe
Conduct withall; but they entertained thoſe Meſſengers as they
had done the former, threatening to whip one, whom they tooke
along with them; and ſent us word, that if wee had any thing to
ſay to them, wee ſhould come to them, and wee ſhould have juſtice
there, and that if wee came with force, they would meet us half the
way.   Our meſſengers returning with theſe ſcornfull anſwers, the
Court reſolved to ſend ſome force to fetch them in; and in the
mean time there came a ſecond letter from them;(the Copy whereof
is hereafter alſo ſet downe) but before wee ſent forth our ſouldiers,
wee wrote to them to this effect: *Viz.*   That although the injuries
and provocations wee had indured from them were very grievous,
yet that our Juſtice and moderation might appeare to all men, wee
had condeſcended ſo farre to their owne propoſition, as wee would
ſend ſome Commiſſioners to them, to heare their anſwers and alle-
gations, and if thereupon they would give us ſuch ſatisfaction as
ſhould bee juſt, wee would leave them in peace; if otherwiſe, wee
would right our ſelves by force of Armes: And ſignified withall,
                                                              that

that wee would ſend a ſufficient guard with our Commiſſioners; for
ſeeing they would not truſt themſelves with us upon our ſafe conduct, wee had no reaſon to truſt any of ours with them upon their
bare curteſie. Accordingly about a week after wee ſent three Commiſſioners, and 40 Muſqueteers with them, with inſtructions, firſt
to ſpeak and treate with them, and to require ſatisfaction according
to Juſtice, and if it were denyed, then to take them by force, and
bring them priſoners to *Boſton*; and to take withall ſo much of their
ſubſtance as ſhould ſatisfie our charges. By the way as they went
they met with another letter from them, letting them know , that
they feared them not, but were prepared for them: And accordingly they had fortified themſelves in one houſe (ſome 12 of them)
and had lined the walls with earth (Musket proofe) and had made
Flanckers, and provided victualls, &c. to indure a ſiege. So that
when our Commiſſioners came to the place, they would admit no
parly. But after a while, by the mediation of ſome of their neighbours, they were content to parley, and offered to referre the cauſe
to Arbitrators,ſo as ſome of them might bee of *Providence* , or of
Roade Iſland. Our Commiſſioners were content to ſend to us
to know our minds about it, and in the meane time ſate ſtill. Such
of the Court as could meet, returned anſwer that their Propoſition
was neither ſeaſonable nor reaſonable, nor could it bee ſafe or honourable for us to accept thereof : 1 Becauſe they would never
offer nor hearken to any termes of agreement before our ſouldiers
had them in their power. 2 Becauſe the ground of their Propoſition was falſe, for wee were not parties (as they pretended) but
equall Judges between the *Indians* and others who were complai-
nants, and themſelves, (and yet in a caſe of warre, parties may bee
Judges.) 3 They were no State, or Body politique, but a few
fugitives living without Law or Government, and ſo not honourable for us to joyne with them in ſuch a way of reference. 4 The
parties whom they would referre it unto,were ſuch as had been rejected by us, and all the Governments in the Country, and ſo not
likely to bee equall to us, nor able to judge of the cauſe: and their
blaſphemous and reproachfull writings, &c. were not matters fit
to bee compoſed by Arbitrement, (being deeply criminall) but either to bee purged away by repentance and publique ſatisfaction, or
elſe by publique puniſhment. For theſe and other reaſons, the
Commiſſioners were required to proceed according to their Inſtructions.

ctions. And thereupon they intrenched themfelves about the houfe, and in few dayes forced them to yeeld, and fo brought them to *Bofton*, where they were kept in prifon till the Court fate, and had their dyet from the Cookes (as good meat and drinke as the Towne afforded.) The next Lords day they refufed to goe to the Church affembly, except they might have liberty to fpeake there, as occafion fhould be. They were anfwered by fome of the Magiftrates that it appertained to the Elders to order the affairs of the Church, but they might prefuppofe they fhould not bee denyed fuch liberty, fpeaking words of truth and foberneffe. So in the afternoon they came, and were placed in a convenient feate before the Elders. Mr. *Cotton* the Teacher taught then (in his ordinary courfe) out of *Acts* 19. of *Demetrius* fpeech for *Diana* her filver fhrine. After Sermon *Gorton* defired leave to fpeake, which being granted, hee tooke occafion from the Sermon to fpeake to this effect, That in the Church now there was nothing but Chrift, fo that all our Ordinances, Minifters, and Sacraments, &c. were but mens inventions, for fhew and pomp, and no other then thofe filver fhrines of *Diana*. He faid alfo, that if Chrift lives eternally, then he died eternally, and other fpeeches of like kinde. And indeed it appeareth both by his fpeeches and letters, that it was his opinion, that Chrift was incarnate in *Adam*, and was that image of God, wherein *Adam* was created ; and that the chiefe worke and merit lay in his *Inanition*, when he became fuch a thing, fo meane, &c. and that his being borne after of the Virgin *Mary*, and fuffering, &c. was but a manifeftation of his fuffering, &c. in *Adam*. Another of them faid that the Sabbath was Chrift, and fo was borne of the Virgin *Mary*. They called Magiftracy among Chriftians an Idol; yet they did acknowledge a Magiftracy in the world to bee fubjected to as an Ordinance of God, but onely as naturall; as the father over his wife and children, and an hereditary Prince over his fubjects.

Their firft appearance before the Court was upon the Lecture day at *Bofton*, before a very great Affembly, where firft the Governour declared the caufe and manner of all the proceedings againft them, and their Letters were openly read, and they had liberty to object, and anfwers were given, as followeth:

Firft, to their plea, That they were not within our Jurifdiction; it was anfwered: 1 If they were not within ours, yet they were within the Jurifdiction of one of our confederates, who had referred
red

red them to us.   2 If they were within no Jurifdiction, then was
there none to complaine to for redreffe of our injuries in way of
ordinary Juftice, and then we had no way of relief but by force of
Armes.

Secondly, to their plea *Of perfecution for their Confcience, &c.* It
was anfwered, that wee did not meddle with them for their opinions, otherwife then they had given us occafion, by their owne Letters and free fpeeches amongft us, for wee wrote to them about civill Controverfies onely, and gave them no occafion to vent their
blafphemies and revilings againft the Ordinances of Religion fet up
with us.

Thirdly, for their title to the *Indians* lands: wee had divers
times defired them to make it appeare; but they alwayes refufed,
even to our Commiffioners, whom (according to their owne
motion) wee fent laft to them: and fince they were in prifon,
wee offered them to fend for any witneffes they would name
to us for that end, but this alfo they refufed.   So that our
title (by the Indians furrender) appeareth good, and having
regained poffeffion, we need not queftion them any further about
that.

Their Letters being read and their Subfcriptions acknowledged,
they were demanded feverally if they would maintaine thofe things
which were contained therein. Their anfwer was, that they would,
in that fenfe they wrote them, and fo were returned to prifon. The
next day they were brought before the Court feverally to be examined upon particulars, (many of the Elders being defired to bee
prefent) becaufe they had faid they could give a good interpretation of every part of their Letters. But the interpretation they gave
being contrary to the words, they were demanded if they would
then retract thofe words, fo plainely different from their pretended
meanings.   But this they refufed to doe, faying, that then they
fhould deny the Truth; for inftance in one or two.   Their Letters were directed, one of them, *To their Neighbours of the Maffachufets*: and the other, *To the great honoured Idoll Generall of the Maffachufets*, and by a meffenger of their owne delivered to our Governour, and many paffages in both Letters particularly applyed to
our Courts, our Magiftrâtes, our Elders, &c. and yet upon their
examinations about their meanings in their reproachfull paffages,
they anfwered that they meant them, of the corrupt eftate of mankinde

kinde in generall, and not of us. So, whereas in their Letter they charged it upon us, as an errour that we teach, *That Chriſt dyed Actually onely*, when he ſuffered under *Pontius Pilate*; and before, onely in *Types*, &c. upon their examination they ſaid, that their meaning was, that his death was actuall to the faith of the Fathers under the Law, (which is in effect the ſame which we hold:) Yet they would not retract their words they had written. The Elders conferred many houres with them before the Court, and by occaſion thereof they diſcovered divers blaſphemous opinions, which they maintained, we will inſtance one which was mentioned before, delivered by *Gorton, viz.* that the Image of God wherein *Adam* was created, was Chriſt; and *Adams* looſing that Image was the death of Chriſt, and the reſtoring of that Image in the Regeneration, was the reſurrection of Chriſt: and ſo the death of him that was borne of the Virgin *Mary* was but a manifeſtation of the former. Maſter *William Tompſon* one of the Elders had ſpent ſome time with them before in the priſon about the opinions which they held forth, and they had profeſſed their agreement with him (for ſubſtance) in every point, ſo as he came to the Court with a purpoſe to ſpeak in their behalf, but when he heard themſelves diſcover thus upon their publique examinations, he ſhewed how he had beene deluded by them. For they excell the *Jeſuites* in the art of equivocation, and regard not how falſe they ſpeake, to all other mens apprehenſions, ſo they keepe to the rules of their owne ſecret intentions. Being asked why they ſpake againſt the Ordinances of the Miniſtery, Sacraments, &c. ſeeing the Scripture allowes them? They anſwered that they were ordained onely for the time of Nonage, but after the Revelation was written, they were to ceaſe, becauſe we finde no mention of them in that booke.

They were unlearned men, the ableſt of them could not write true engliſh, no not in common words, yet they would take upon them to interpret the moſt difficult places of Scripture, and wreſt them any way to ſerve their owne turne. As for inſtance, Mr. *Cotton* preſſing *Gorton* with that in *Act.* 10. Who can forbid water, why theſe ſhould not be baptiſed, &c. He interpreted thus, who can deny but theſe have beene baptiſed, ſeeing they have received the Holy Ghoſt, &c. ſo he allowed them to have beene baptiſed. This ſhift he was put to, that he might maintaine his opinion, *viz:* that ſuch as have beene baptized with the Holy Ghoſt, need not the baptiſme

of

of water.   Divers dayes were fpent both by the Court and the Elders in labouring to bring them to repentance, but all in vaine. They
continued obftinate.   Whereupon they agreed to fentence them,
but firft they brought them in publique before a great Affembly,
and there (out of their Letters and Speeches) they laid upon them
this charge, *viz.* they were found to be blafphemous enemies of the
true Religion of our Lord Jefus Chrift, and of all his holy Ordinances, and likewife of all Civill Government among his people, and
particularly within this jurisdiction.   Then they were demanded,
if they did acknowledge this charge to be juft, and would fubmit
to it, or what exception they had againft it?   They anfwered, they
did not acknowledge it to be juft, but they fell into fome cavilling
fpeeches, fo they were returned unto prifon againe.   Being in prifon they behaved themfelves infolently towards their keeper, and
fpake evill of the Magiftrates, fo as the keeper was forced to threaten
them with Irons, to keepe them quiet.

   After all meanes ufed to reclaime them, and not prevailing, they
were brought before the Court to receive their fentence, which was
this. *Gorton* and fix more of them, were to be fent to feverall townes,
there to bee kept to worke for their livings, and to weare an Iron
chaine upon one leg, and not to depart the limits of the Towne,
nor by word or writing to maintaine any of their blafphemous or
wicked errours upon paine of death, except in conference with any
of the Elders, or any other allowed by fome Magiftrate to conferre
with them; and this to continue during the pleafure of the Court.
Three of the Company (becaufe they had not their hands to the
Letters) were fet at libertie, two of them upon a fmall ranfome as
prifoners taken in warre, and the other, freely, for that he was a-
mongft them in his Mafters houfe, where they were taken; a fourth
being found to be a plaine ignorant young man was difcharged alfo, onely enjoyned to abide a time in one of our Townes, but hee
went away and returned no more, contrary to his promife.   There
were two other who were brought in after; (but not by force) the
one of them difclaiming to have any hand in the Letters, was difcharged prefently; the other was kept a while in prifon, and after
upon his fubmiffion &c. was releafed.

   Gorton and the other fix remained in the feverall Townes all that
Winter; and then in regard of their wives and children (who were
like to be much diftreffed by their husbands abfence) they were fet at
liberty,

liberty, and baniſhed upon paine of death if they were found in a-
ny part of our juriſdiction.

After the Court had paſſed ſentence upon them for their confinement, we ſent to fetch ſo many of their Cattle, as might defray the
charges they had put us to, which amounted to about one hundred
and ſixty pounds, but the Cattle came not to ſo much, for we left
every of them a part for the ſupport of their families, and ſome of
them had no Cattle at all.

The Letters follow,

Mooſhawſet Novemb: **20.** 1642.
To our Neighbours of the Maſſachuſets.

VVHereas we lately received an irregular note, profeſſing its
forme from the Maſſachuſets, with four mens names
ſubſcribed thereunto, as principall authors of it, of the chiefe a-
mongſt you; We could not eaſily give credit to the truth thereof,
not onely becauſe the conveyers of it unto us, are knowne to bee
men, whoſe conſtant and profeſſed acts are worſe, then the coun-
terfeiting of mens hands; but alſo, becauſe we thought that men
of your parts and profeſſion, would never have proſtrated their wiſdome to ſuch an act.   But conſidering that cauſleſſe enmity you
have againſt us; the proofe whereof, every occaſion brings forth;
Wee cannot but conclude, that no act ſo ill which that ancient mother will not bring forth her ſeed unto.   For wee know very well,
that it is the name of Chriſt called upon us, which you ſtrive a-
gainſt; Thence it is that you ſtand on tip-toe, to ſtretch yourſelves beyond your bounds; to ſeeke occaſion againſt us; (So) as you might
hide your ſinne with *Adam*, bearing the world in hand; it is not
your deſire to contend with us; But ſome civill breach in our courſes, which you onely ſeeke to redreſſe.   Whereas neither you, nor
any (in way of truth) can finde wherewith, to bring us under the Cenſure of a diſorderly courſe of walking amongſt
men: And as for the way of that ancient ſpirit of accuſation of
the brethren, we weigh it not, knowing him to be a lyer, (or in the
abſtract, a lye) from the beginning, yea and the father of it alſo;
which thing you cannot know, though it were told unto you.

Whereas you ſay, *Robert Cole*, *William Arnauld* with others, have
put themſelves under the Government and protection of your Juriſdiction

riſdiction, which is the occaſion you have now got to contend; we
wiſh your words were verified, that they were not elſewhere to be
found, being nothing but the ſhame of Religion, Diſquiet, and Di-
ſturbance of the place where they are. For, we know neither the one
nor the other, with all their aſſociates and Confederates, have power to enlarge the bounds, by Kinge *Charles* limited unto you.

Behold therefore in this your act, a Map of your ſpirituall e-
ſtate, (to uſe your owne phraſe) for we know that the Spirituality
of your Churches, is the Civility of your Commonweale, and the
Civility of your Comonwealth, is the ſpirituality of your Churches, the wiſdome of man, being the whole accompliſhment of them
both; of which Tree, you delight dayly to eate (finding it faire and
beautifull) to gaine Conformity with your maker.   In theſe
your Diſſembling ſubjects; groſly profane amongſt us, but full
of the ſpirit of your purity, when they are with you, you may remember the brand your ſelves have ſet upon ſome of them, the Cauſe
wherof was never yet removed, though it abide not upon their
backe; Nor yet the Cauſe of your Commitment of them unto *Sathan* according unto your Law, for if that were removed, you
ſhould doe them wrong, in not reſuming your vomit into its former Concoction againe; Nor are we ignorant of thoſe diſgracefull
tearmes they uſe, and give out againſt you, behind your backes,
their ſubmiſſion therefore can bee to no other end, but to ſatisfie
their owne luſts, not onely conceived, but in violent motion, a-
gainſt their Neighbours, who never offered the leaſt wrong unto
them, only the propoſition of Amity, is object ſufficient, for theſe
mens enmitie.

Even ſo the paſſions of ſin, which are by the Law, having force
in your Members; you going about with great labour and in-
duſtry to ſatisfie them by your ſubmiſſion unto the word of God,
in your Faſting, and feaſting, in Contributing, and treaſuring, in
retiredneſſe for Study, and bowing of the backes of the poore, going forth in labour to maintaine it, and in the ſpirit of that hireling,
raiſing up, your whole ſtructure and edifice, in all which you
bring forth nothing but fruit unto death, ſome labouring for a price
to give for the keeping of their ſoules, in peace and ſafe eſtate and
Condition, and ſome to have their bodies furniſhed with riches, honour and eaſe, and further then the Lord Jeſus agrees with theſe,
you mind him not, nay you renounce and reject him, and with
theſe

thefe (according to your Acceptation and practice) he holds no
Correfpondency at all, being the Confultation and operation of
that his onely adverfarie, man being that which you depend uppon, and not the Lord, Crying out in way of Elevation, and ap-
lauding his minifters, when in the meane time, you know not what,
nor who they are, profeffing them under a mediate Call of Chrift,
though formerly, they have beene Called immediately by him, her-
by fhowing your felves to be thofe, that deftroy the Sacred ordinance of God: For if you make Chrift to be that to day, in ftate-
ing his minifters; which he was not yefterday, and that in the
tyme of the Gofpell alfo, (to fpeake acording to your Law) to be
found in them both, you therin affirm, that he hath beene that to
his minifters, which now he is not, and to make the Son of God to
have beene that which now he is not, is to make a Nullitie of
him, not to be at all, for he is the Lord that changeth not, no not
a fhadow therof is found in him, fo that you plainely Crucifie unto your felves, the Lord of glory, and put him to an open fhame;
So that as you know not, how Chrift, converfing with his
father in heaven, is found on the earth, amongft the true wor-
fhippers, no more do you know, how in his converfing with *Ni-
codemus* on the earth, he concludes himfelfe to be in heaven, with
his father. On this foundation hangeth the whole building of
your Doctrine, concerning the fufferings of Chrift, you Annihilate
the Crofs, then the which, the Saints have no other Confolation:
and prepare no better a place then Purgatory, for the honourable
fathers of our Lord: For you conclude, that Chrift dyed in the Decree, and purpofe God, in the time of the Law, but actually onely
when he hanged on the Croffe in the dayes of *Herod* and *PontiusPi-
late*, that hee was crucified in the types and fhadowes of the law, but
in the truth, and fubftance, when hee appeared borne of the Virgin
Mary: So muft you alfo conclude that the fathers under the law,
were only faved, in purpofe and Decree, in Type and fhadow, but
actually and fubftantially onely at the Comming of Chrift in the
flefh: therefore deale plainely with thofe that depend upon you for
inftruction (as your Anceftours in the papacie have don) and pro-
claime a place of purgatorie, provided for them in the meane, without which, your Doctrine hath no foundation. For if you raife up
a fhaddow, without a fubftance, and the fubftance of him that dwel-
leth in light, without a fhaddow, you play the part of Wifards, or
Necromancers,

[Errata: read *Maffachufets* instead of *Bofton* in the head-lines to page 37.]

[Errata, l. 27, read purpofe of God.]

Necromancers, not the part of true Naturalifts, in the things of the Kingdome of god.

So that as farre as thefe men are from beinge honourable and loyall fubjects, fo farre are you from being voluntaries in the Day of Gods power, and from yeelding fubjection unto the Beauties of holinefs.   Such alfo is your profeffed Rule, and Government, in the things that concern the Kingdom of our God, they are infinitly beyond, and out of the Reach of that Spirit which is gone out a- mongft you, the Capacity whereof can no wayes comprehend, the breadth of the land of *Emanuel,* nor entreth it within the Vale, There- fore it cannot know thofe Cherubims of glory, neither can it heare the voice of that lively Oracle, fpeaking onely from off the covering Mercy-feate, and not elfewhere to be heard; We fpeake not but what wee know, thefe things are out of its Jurifdiction; Therefore dumb in telling Juftice, nor fpeakes it any of that Righteoufneffe and glory, compryfed in another circuit, then ever you were yet made Lords of: Long therfore may you boaft, of your Jurifdiction before ever you attaine unto a *Jurisprudentia,* in thefe things.

In that you tell us wee offer you wrong, by a pretended purchafe: you are as much miftaken in the purchafe, as in the wrong, For it is right that we are about to do, neither is our purchafe a pretence, but precedentiall, not onely in this Civill refpect, but may alfo admonifh all men, to take heed, how they depend upon falfe and felf-feeking interpreters, when both themfelves, and they that have the vifion, are ignorant of the Contract, and Covenant of God.   Thence it is, that you teach, that the fpoufe of Chrift, upon Contract with her Lord, may conceive the feed of immortalitie, and bring forth fruit unto God, when as yet the day of mariage, that great Feaftivitie, and folemnization, of the Confolations of God, is not yet comne, witneffe your prorogation thereof, if not to the Defcenfion of Chrift from heaven unto the earth, to Raigne certaine years, yet to the Calling of the Jewes, whom yee your felves are, according to the flefh, and to the deftruction of that Man of finn whom yee fo ftoutly maintain, What is this, but to pro- claime   unto all the world, that Audacious fpirit of whore- doms, profeffing Conception and bringing forth before the Nup- tiall day?

In that you conclude your Clyents Right to arife out of foure years poffeffion, wee have no fuch order, if you meane the Right
of

of Conqueſt, (onely held in that tenure) the true owners were never yet ſubdued, for that is the right they expect to injoy by you,
for ſome of them committed part of their ſuppoſed right unto us,
profeſſing it was, that they might have help, to injoy the reſt; But
when they ſaw, wee would not be Abetters unto them without,
much leſſe contrary unto Covenant, then they flye unto you for
help, Their poſſeſſion, beeing a meere intruſion, as all the Natives
know and ever exclaymed againſt them for the ſame, And ſo may
our Countrymen alſo, whoſe eyes are not dazled with envie, and
eares open to Lyes, as we know yours are, elſe you had heard both
ſydes ſpeake, before you had Judged.

But wee profeſs right held, according to no ſuch intereſt, but
upon the ground of Covenant onely, knowne in its nature; In the
parties 'twixt whom it is plight, In the poſſeſſer, and the poſſeſſed,
with the nature of all fruit ariſing from their accord and concur-
rencie, together with their Diſtinct, Harmonicall, Reciprocall, and
Joint properties, and operations of them both: Such is the tenure
wee hould, and maintain, before men and Angels, and oppoſe it
againſt man and Divell, Not in taking up unto our ſelves, certaine
offices and officers which wee can teach children to bee, and to perform, and from thence preſently to conclude, the poſſeſſion of the
Kingdome, Crying out our peace offerings are upon us, this Day
we have payd our vowes. But when that Dark cloud deſcended upon the Tabernacle, becomes the light, and glory of all Iſraell
(there being nothing acknowledged amongſt them, but what ari-
ſeth out thence) then, and then only, are the orders, as alſo the
men of Iſraell, derived from the true fountaine, which no tongue
can confeſs, but it is ſalvation, and then, not elſe, is the heritage
of our Lord in poſſeſſion, yea, even the waylefs wilderneſſ knowes,
how to afford them an habitation, which had its being before the hills and mountaines were borne: which men begin
to flye unto for refuge, to hide them from the preſence of the Lamb:
this is a poſſeſſion, which no man can intrude himſelfe into: it is
onely Covenanted with him, thorow an inlightned eye, and boa-
red eare, which man performeth not, nor can it be received from
him.

For wee know that Cloud of thick darkneſſe, that hides and co-
vers the whole frame and fabrick of the work of God, to be the clee-
ring and evidencing of every point and particular thereof :yea to us,

it

it is even that cloud of witneſs, which teſtifies unto us, the like
workes to appeare, when ever the world hath occaſion to make uſe
of us.

Never doth it ſhine but in the night, never is it dark to Iſrael but
in the day, but in the one, and the other, the only glory and ſaftie
of all the tribes: but how, you know not, nor can you with all your
libraries, give the interpretation thereof, but have loſt it in the wil-
derneſs, and accordingly, have made the whole way, and will of
our Lord, the ouldneſſe of the letter, both to your ſelves, and to all
that have an eare to liſſen unto you; Thence it is that the day of
Lord, is a day of Darkneſs and Gloomineſs unto you, but of Joy
and gladneſs unto us; yea, it lifts up our head onely, and then
is our ſalvation neere; For wee know the worthies of *David*
doubled about the bed of *Solomon* , which expell all feare in the
night , handling the ſword with ſuceſs , making the adverſaries
nothing but meat to feede upon, ſo that the tyme of your feares
is the time of our Courage and Conqueſt , for when you feare
errour, ſchiſme, Rents and Confuſions in Church and ſtate, then do
wee know the Meſſenger of the Covenant, the Lord whom wee ſeek
is ſpeeding his paſſage into his holy temple: For who (under the
terrors of your ſpirit) may abide his Coming, hee being like a refi-
ners fire, and Fullers ſope ?

[Errata: l. 11,
read. day of
the Lord.]

In that you invite us unto your Courts to fetch your equall bal-
lanced juſtice, upon this ground, that you are becomne one with
our adverſaries, and that, both in what they have, and what they
are, and wee know them to bee ſuch, as profeſs the day of the Lord
an unhallowed thing.   Now, if wee have our opponant, to prefer
his action againſt us, and not only ſo, but to bee our Counſell, our
Jurie, and our Judg, for ſo it muſt bee, if you bee one with them (as
you affirm) wee know before hand, how our Cauſe will bee ended,
and ſee the ſcale of your equall Juſtice turned alreadie, before wee
have layd our Cauſe therein, and cannot but admire, to ſee you ca-
ried ſo contrarie to your owne received principles: For you
know not how to finde Chriſt as a Ruling and teaching Elder
both in one perſon, therfore he is not Complete amongſt you by
your owne law, except in ſeverall perſons, and you may thank tra-
dition, elſe you know no more how to finde both a king and a
prieſt in him, and yet in your way of making tender of your Juſtice
unto us you know how to become one with our adverſaries (ſo) as

if

if wee deale with them, wee deale with you, and if wee have to doe
with you, wee have to doe with them alſo, yea further, wee know,
that the chiefe amongſt you, have profeſſed wee are not worthy to
live; and that if ſome of us were amongſt you, wee ſhould hardly
ſee the place of our abode any more; Now that they have brooded
upon their law, to take away life, they muſt much more bring it up,
in taking away all means of life, Witnes our prohibition, that no
powder ſhould befould unto us for our money, and that in a time
when you could not thinke your ſelves ſafe, in all your owne, ſelf
proviſion and worldly furniture , except youdiſarmed a company
of poor Indians, whom *Aaron* **your** Leviticall Sacrificer hath made
Naked, as hee doth all thoſe which triumph in a Calf, though the
moſt coſtly and beautifull, that the Jewells and eare-rings of Learning, either in Language, or art, can poſſibly bring forth: your
owne amazements upon meer Rumors, may teſtifie the truth hereof;
ſo then; wee are Judged by your law before our Cauſe bee hard, or
our ſelves brought forth under the liberties of it, which thing is
well pleaſing unto us , to have our Condition conformed unto
Moſes the man of God, who was dead in *Pharaohs* account, before he
was brought forth, and ſo it was with Chriſt our lord, in the dayes
of *Herod* alſo, who is our life (at which you ſtrike) and makes
all things, yea, Death it ſelf, lively, and advantagious unto us.

Wee cannot but wonder, that you ſhould read the Scripture, and
not finde them fulfilled, in, and amongſt your ſelves, when as they
appeare ſo apparantly, that he that runs may read them:what think
you of *Herod*, when the Lord had delivered *Peter* out of priſon, and
releaſed him of thoſe bonds, and brought him from that thraldom,
which he had ſo Cruelly impoſed upon him, to gaine the favour of
the Jewes , and that by a power ſupereminent, tranſcending the
bounds of his authoritie, and by a wiſdom ſurpaſſing the Depth of
his Counſell, and policie, to fynd out, together with his ſouldiers
and Champions , he preſently goes downe to *Ceſarea* , and *Herod*
is angry with them of *Tyrus* & *Sidon*, (*thumomachon*)a heavieFriend,
or hath a ſecret grudg or perturbation of mind , manifeſted in an
outreaching , and circumventing policie , to ſubdue them unto
himſelf, that he might Rule over them: Finding himſelf fall ſhort
of power and policie, to ſubject the word of God in the meſſinger
of it, to ſatisfy his owne luſts, in his lordſhip over it, he purſues
with all egarneſſe to make himſelf a god, by Raigning over the bodies

dies and eſtates of men; yea, though they be but ſuch, as *Tyrus* and *Sidon,* can afford unto him, to make ſubjects of, and when they come unto him with one accord to make offer of themſelves, in yeelding to his affectionate and politicall project, he ſitting uppon the Judgment ſeate, in his Royall apparell, making his oration, of what power he hath to protect them, what wiſdom and Counſell, to miniſter Juſtice and righteouſneſs unto them (which office belongs only unto the Lord) the people with a ſhout crying out, the voice of god and not of man, the truth and ſubſtance of which Cry is, this is the ordinance of god and not of man, immediately the angel of the Lord ſmites him, and hee that ever acknowledged himſelf, to bee a worme, and no man upon the earth, Conſumes and eates up all his pomp and glory, even as thoſe, whom you account the Shame and Contempt of the people, ſhall (thorow that angell of the Covenant) waſte and bring to nought all thoſe Rhetoricall, (though earthly) Orations that are made amongſt you, by your ſo Learned, ſtudious, and experienced Clarkes: take for illuſtration of your eſtate as above, the ſpeech of your alderman *Oliver,* in caſe of committing *Francis Hutchinſon* to priſon; one of your Churchmembers wondering that brother *Winthrop* would do it before the Church had dealt with him, Brother, ſaith hee, why; hee is thy god man.

Lend your eye yet farther, to parallell your practiſe perſonated in *Pylate* and the people, when *Pylat* offereth Jeſus unto, the people to be judged, they profeſs, they have ſuch a law, as puts no man to Death: they are all for mercy and forgiveneſs, when they are out of the Judgment hall, but let *Pylat* enter in thither; and then, nothing but Crucifie him, Crucifie him; be their accuſations, and witneſſes, never ſo falſe: even ſo, in your dealings with men, in way of your Jewiſh brotherhood, your law is all for mercie, to Redreſs, reform, and for preſervation, both of ſoule and bodie; Do but enter into the Common hall, and then, as *Pylat* asked (am I a Jew?) ſo do you, Doe I ſit, or ſpeake here, as a brother?   I tro not, I am now in a higher ſphere, then that (though they be acknowledged coheirs with Chriſt) can ataine unto, therfore if witneſs be brought in, and Oath taken, though never ſo untrue, your conſciences are purged by law, and your power muſt have tribute payd unto it, ſo far as mens Names, to bee branded with infamie, eſtates, depryving women and children of things neceſſarie, and precious lives of men

can

can extend themſelves, to contribute any thing thereunto; ſo that the profeſſed mercie, and Clemencie of your law, to exerciſe cenſures only for amendment of life, and recoverie, comes unto this iſſue, as much as in you lies,to ſend both ſoule and body downe unto hell for ever without redreſſe, and all hope of recovery.

But your houre, and the power of Darkneſſe, is known what it is,either to have mens perſons in admiration becauſe of advantage; or elſe, to ſeek all occaſions againſt them, to brand them with all manner of reproch, and ignominie, but for the truth, taught daily in the Temple, you know not how to ſtreatch out your hand, or exerciſe your miniſtry againſt it, left it become leprous, and you take it back again with loſſe, when it appeares dried and withered.

And wherefore reaſon yee amongſt your ſelves, ſaying, wee exerciſe the power of your miniſtrations againſt none but ſuch as are Delinquents, whereby we cleer the innocent, and eſtabliſh peace in all our borders?

Wee demand, what think you of thoſe two witneſſes, prophecying in Sackcloth, a thouſand two hundreth and threeſcore Dayes: thoſe two olive trees,and two candleſtickes,ſtanding before the God of the earth? are theſe guiltie and vile perſons, out of whoſe hands (by the power of your miniſtries) you are delivering and releaſing the world? then indeed are your wayes juſtifiable: But if theſe bee the Juſt, Choſen, and peculiar friends of God, yea ſuch, as without which, his truth and Righteouſneſſe are not juſtified, his wiſdom, and holineſſe maintained and upheld in the world, in point of ſalvation by Chriſt, then are your wayes wicked, and to bee abhorred; for in your profeſſed Courſe, you are they, by whom theſe are ſlaine, and put to Death, and all your glory is to keepe their Corpes unburied in your ſtreetes, and yet you know not what you are doing, no more then you know what theſe witneſſes are, whom you are altogether ignorant of, for your Libraries never ſaw them, and you ſee not but by their eyes, for theſe are two,and never more, nor yet leſſe,yea ever the ſame,they are olive trees,elſe no witneſſes, and alſo Candleſticks, elſe both the former faile, yea, are not at all. Wee muſt tell you what theſe are, elſe wee cannot declare how you kill them, for it is not our intent to open unto you the houſe of the treaſures, the ſilver and the gold, and the ſpices, and the precious oyntment, nor the houſe of our armour, becauſe you take all as

execra-

execrable, and put all to a profane uſe that commeth from us; but theſe two witneſſes are the life and death of our Lord Jeſus; or, in the true language of heaven alſo, the ſtrength and the weakneſſe of Chriſt, for hee was crucified through weakneſſe, but hee liveth by the power of God: this is the word of the Lord in *Zerubbabel*, Not by an army, nor by power, and ſo deprives him of all ſtrength, but by aſpirit, that the greateſt mountaine, or loftieſt hill in the world cannot ſtand before, but becomes a plaine, which with facility and eaſe hee paſſeth upon; thence it is that hee doth not onely lay the top or the head ſtone of all, but alſo the loweſt in the foundation, and then onely is the voice of ſhouting heard, Grace, grace in the houſe for ever; and then doth the day of ſmall things become the day of joy and triumph, yea, of parting the rich ſpoiles and prey of all the world, for then hee that doth but turn and lift up his eyes he cannot looke beſides that great flying book of the Curſe that is gone forth over the whole earth.

Without theſe two witneſſes jointly uttering themſelves in every particular Scripture undertaken to bee divulged by any, no evidence nor teſtimony of God is given, or brought in at all, but a meere refuge of lies for the ſoules of men to betake themſelves unto; without theſe two pipes of the olive trees emptying themſelves into the bowle of the candleſticks, no unction nor oyle at all is found in them, and that being wanting, the light of the Sanctuary is gone out; ſo that the light appearing amongſt you is onely the light of *Balaam,* whoſe eye was open, which you may read either *Shethum* or *Sethum,* for that opening is nothing elſe but the ſhutting up of the holy things of God, ſo that in ſeeing you ſee not, but communicate onely in the light of that beaſt, who puts the witneſſes to death, as *Balaam* did in the ſight of that dumbe beaſt of his whoſe eyes were opened to ſee the angel before him; ſo that while you thinke it is our wiſdome to ſtoope unto you for light, wee never come amongſt you but ſee our ſelves in a regiment of groſſe and palpable darkneſſe, and diſcern you very plainly, how you ſcrabble upon the wall to finde the doore of *Lots* houſe, and cannot. As alſo how you toil yourſelves to climbe up into the ſheep-fold, another, yea, ſo many other wayes, and have no ſight nor diſcerning of us the Door, at all, by the which whoſoever entereth, becomes a true feeder of the flock of God; yea, none entereth in thereat, but the true Shepheard himſelf.

Moſt

Moft impious it is to put to death two fuch Noble witneffes, that
have power to fhut heaven that it raine not in the dayes of their
prophecying; to turne the waters into bloud, and to fmite the earth
with all manner of plagues as oft as they wil,whom that fpirit that
is amongft you kills on this wife, the life or power of the fonne of
God, as above, which is infinite, not admitting of circumfcri-
ption or containment, for the heaven of heavens cannot containe
him,yet have you not dared to grafpe and inviron that power in the
heavens, and therefore have refolved and concluded that hee onely
rules upon the earth in thefe dayes by his Deputies, Lievtenants,
and Vicegerents, whereby you limit, and fo deftroy the holy One
of Ifrael; for give him that in one time, or place, which afterwards,
or elfewhere you deny him, and you make a nullity of him unto
your felves, and in fo doing, you kill that other witneffe, namely,
the death or weakneffe of the Lord Jefus: for you muft have man
to bee honourable, learned, wife, experienced, and of good report,
elfe they may not rule among you; yea and thefe things are of
man, and by man, as appeares, in that they onely officiate fo, as
man may difanull and take it away againe; witneffe your change of
officers, conftantly fpeaking for us herein; thus have you flaine
alfo the death or the weakneffe of Chrift, who profeffeth himfelfe
to bee a worm and no man, the fhame and contempt of the people;
and thefe faithfull and true witneffes thus flaine, you muft of neceffity deny buriall, and keep them both in open view in your ftreets,
or otherwife all your pompe and glory falls to the duft whence it
came, and on which it feeds.   Nor can you fend your prefents one
to another of your acts of Juftice, power to protect, wealth, honour, and friends wherewith you gratifie each other; and where
thefe are thus flaine, and their corps lie in open view, none of the
gentiles, peoples, tongues, and kindreds fuffering their carkaffes to
bee put in graves,there is that great City which fpiritually is *Sodom*
and *Egypt,*where our Lord is crucified; but after three dayes and an
half, the fpirit of life from God fhall enter into them, and they fhal
ftand up upon their feet to the terrour of you all: Nor doe you
thinke that wee onely inveigh againft the great ones of this world
for thus doing, for wee know that the bafeft peafant hath the fame
fpirit with the greateft Princes of this world, and the greateft of the
Princes of this world, hath the very fame fpirit wherewith the
bafeft peafant hath laid himfelfe open in the view of all men: thefe
                                                              wee

wee fay, are the two witneſſes if you can receive it, and what a difhonour is it to trade fo much by meanes of witneſſes, and yet not
know what a true witneſſe is? which if you did, you durſt not attempt the things you doe, whereby you caſt reproach upon all the
world, in that you profeſſe your felves a choice people pickt out of
it, and yet goe on, in fuch practices as you doe, maintaining them
as your onely glory.   Our Lord gives you in charge not to fweare
at all, but it is your dignity to bring men to your feates of Juſtice
with nothing but oathes in their mouthes, why doe you not bal-
lance the fcriptures in this point? *viz.*

It hath beene faid of old, Thou ſhalt not committ adultery, but
I fay unto you, hee that looketh on a woman to luſt after her, hath
committed adultery with her in his heart already : fo alfo it hath
beene fayd of old, Thou ſhalt not forfweare thy felf, but I fay unto
you, fweare not at all: fo that if it be adulterie, to looke to luſt, it
is alfo forfwearing a mans felf, to fweare at all; if the one be adultery,
the other is perjury, if one be admitted in fome cafes, the otheralfo,
fo that in preaching the toleration, nay the duty of an oath, you
preach the toleration, yea the duty of adulterie it felf; So that our
Lord plainly evinceth unto all mens confciences, not onely the guilt
but the folly and madneſſe of the oath of man, ſhewing how farre
it is, either from inveſting into place, or demonſtrating Caufes, fo
that hee that concludeth upon honour, and power, received from
the oath of man, or upon knowledge and bouldneſs, to judge in
a caufe, from that teſtimony without the which he.could not have
it, is as vaine in his thoughts, as if hee ſhould herupon conclude, I
have now altered the frame of heaven, which is no lefs ſtable then
the throne of the great God, or demoliſhed the earth, which is as
firme as his foot-ſtoole for ever, or made a fraction in the orders of
Jerufalem, that choice and peculiar City of the great King, whofe
inſtitutions no mortall breath can intrench upon, or to profeſſe his
authority and skill to be fuch, whereby he can make a haire of his
head blacke or white, caufe his age to wax old as doth a garment,
or renew it with the Eagle at his pleafure, hereby doth man (in this
point of fwearing) profeſſe his folly to bee fuch, that hee is become
not onely vaine in his imaginations, but unto that pride and ufur-
pation therein, as to intrude himfelfe into the prerogative royall of
hisMaker.

So that however you boaſt of the Ordinances of God, yet he tels
                                                                    you

you there is no more then yea, yea, and nay, nay, in them, for what is once nay, is ever nay in the Ordination of Chrift, and what is once yea, is ever yea with him, and according to his account however man reckoneth, whofe account fhall be called over againe, what is once curfe, is ever the curfe, and what is once the principality and power of Chrift, is ever the principality and power of Chrift, as that which is once the principality and power of Darkeneffe, is ever the fame, what hands foever it cometh into for manifeftation: meafure your kingdome whether it bee eternall, and your Jurifdiction whether it bee illimited, for he hath given (him) the heathen for his inheritance, the utmoft parts of the earth for his poffeffion, and a kingdome of leffe extent hee profeffeth not, nor can hee approve or acknowledge any that doe, no more then light can approve of darkeneffe, or the Lord *Jehovah* of the Lord *Baal.*

Bee wife therefore, and bethinke your felves while it is called to day, harden not your hearts, as though you would make your felves *Meriba*, nothing but ftrife and contention againft the Lord, rather kiffe the fonne (if it bee poffible) left his wrath bee kindled and you perifh from the way for ever, O bleffed onelythey, that hope in him.

So that hee which profeffeth on this wife, it is yea, I am a paftour, but it was nay, at fuch a time I was none, hee renounceth that fpirit of the true paftour, yet onely feeder of Ifrael, profeffing onely that fpirit that pufheth the weake with the horne, and pudleth with his feet the waters where the flocke ofGod fhould drinke. Hee with whom it is yea, I am a Ruler, but it was nay when I was none at all, renounceth that fpirit of him that rules in righteoufneffe, profeffing the fpirit of him that rules according to the god of this world, that Prince of the power of the Aire, who is now working fo effectually in the children of difobedience. So alfo hee with whom it is yea, I am a Captaine, or chiefe flaughter-man,but it was nay, time was I was none at all,renounceth that victorie and flaughter made by the Captaine and High-prieft of our profeffion, (who as hee is a Lambe flaine from the beginning, his victory and flaughter muft bee of the fame antiquity,) profeffing himfelfe to bee a chiefe flaughter-man, or fuperfluous Giant, made in that hoaft of the Philiftims, ftanding in readineffe to come out, to defie the hoaft of the living God: yea, it is evident, that whatfoever is more then yea,yea,and nay,nay,not fettlingeach upon itsBafe,whereon it ftan-
deth

deth for ever without controule, but can remove, create,or make
void offices and officers at their pleafure, is of that evill, or not of
Jefus, the falvation of his people, but of *Shedim* that wafter and de-
ftroyer of mankinde for ever: know therefore that it is the oath of
God which confirmes and makes good his Covenant and promife
unto a thoufand generations: and it is the oath of man, which is
the bond and obligation of that league and agreement made with
death and hell for ever; bee yee affured it is not the tabernacle
of witnes which you have amongft you,brought in by Jefus into the
poffeffion of the Gentiles, but it is *Siccuth* your King, or the tabernacle of *Molock*, the ftarre of your God *Remphan*, figures which
you have made unto your felves, which you have taken up, and are
bearing fo ftoutly upon your fhoulders. Now to tell you what an
oath according to God is, that the fcriptures are delivered upon
no other ground or termes of certainty, where ever they are divulged, is a thing out of your jurifdiction, you cannot difcerne or
judge of it, therefore according to our word above, wee leave it as
a parable unto you, as all the holy word of our God is, as your converfation in all points, as in this,daily declareth.

In a word, when wee have to doe in your jurifdiction, we know
what it is to fubmit to the wife difpenfations of our God, when
you have to doe amongft us, in the liberties hee hath given unto us,
wee doubt not, but you fhall finde him judge amongft us, beyond
and above any caufe or thing you can propofe unto us; And let
that fuffice you,and know, that you cannot maintaine a jurifdiction, but you muft reject all inroades upon other mens priviledges,
and fo doe wee.

In the meane time, wee fhall (as wee thinke good) bee calling o-
ver againe fome matters that you have taken up and had the handling of them amongft you, to fee what juftice or equity wee finde
hath beene exercifed in them, and redreffe them accordingly: for
wee profeffe right unto all men,and not to doe any violence at all,as
you in your prefcript threaten to doe to us, for wee have learned
how to difcipline our children, or fervants, without offering violence unto them, even fo doe wee know how to deale with our deboift, rude, nay inhumane Neighbours, (or if you will, Nabals)
without doing violence, but rather rendring unto them that which
is their due.

Nor fhall wee deprive a witneffe of his modeft teftimony for the
outcries,

out-cries, and clamours of fuch a one as ill bred apoftatized *Arnauld*
that fellonious Hog-killer, being the partie to bee teftified againft,
or for the oath of any interefted in the caufe, nor fhall wee bee
forward to come fo farre, to finde your worke upon your requeft,
till wee know you to beare another minde, then others of your
Neighbours doe, with whom wee have had to doe in this country,
whofe pretended and devifed Lawes wee have ftooped under, to the
robbing and fpoiling of our goods, the livelyhood of our wives
and children, thinking they had laboured, (though groping in
great darkeneffe) to bring forth the truth, in the rights and equity of things, but finding them to bee a company of groffe diffembling hypocrites, that under the pretence of Law and Religion,
havedone nothing elfe, but gone about to eftablifh themfelves in
wayes to maintaine their owne vicious lufts, wee renounce their
Diabolicall practice, being fuch as have denyed in their publique
Courts, that the lawes of our Native Country fhould bee named
amongft them, yea thofe ancient ftatute lawes, cafting us into moft
bafe naftie and infufferable places of imprifonment for fpeaking according to the language of them, in the meane while, breaking o-
pen our houfes in a violent way of hoftilitie (abufing our wives and
our little ones) to take from us the volumes wherein they are pre-
ferved, thinking thereby to keepe us ignorant of the courfes they
are refolved to run, that fo the viciofity of their owne wills might
bee a law unto them, yea they have endeavoured, and that in publique expreffions, that a man being accufed by them, fhould not
have liberty to anfwer for himfelfe in open Court. Dealings of
like nature wee finde in the place whereof you ftile us your neighbours, (on whofe unbridled malice, wee finde a higher then you
putting a curbe) and yet in your account and reckoning wee are
the parties that ftill are doing the wrong, and muft beare the guilt
in your moft mature fentence, in whomfoever the fpot arifeth and
abideth. But the God of vengeance (unto whom our caufe is referred, never having our protector and Judge to feeke) will fhew himfelfe in our deliverance out of the hands of you all, yea all the houfe
of that *Ifhbofheth* and *Mephibofheth*, nor will he faile us to utter and
make knowne his ftrength (wherein wee ftand) to ferve in our age,
and to minifter in our Courfe, to day and to morrow, and on
the third day, can none deprive us of perfection, for hee hath taught
us to know what it is to walke to day, and to morrow, and the day
following

following alſo, when a periſhing eſtate cannot ariſe out of *Jeruſa-lem*, though ſhe be the onely one,(yea,none but ſhe) that kills the Prophets and ſtones them that are ſent unto her.

Behold yee that are looking after, and foretelling ſo much of the comming of Chriſt, driving the day before you ſtill for certaine yeares, which ſome (you ſay) ſhall attaine unto, and unto the day of death for the reſt, You blinde guides, as your fathers have ever done, ſo doe yee.   Behold wee ſay, when ever hee appeareth,your houſe (which yee ſo glory in) ſhall bee left unto you deſolate, it ſhall be turned into nothing but deſolation and confuſion, for *Babel* is its name; Nor ſhall you ſee him to your comfort in the glory of his kingdome, untill you can ſay, Bleſſed is hee that commeth in the name of the Lord, when the authority and power of man ap-peares to bee the building of *Babel* unto you, and the name and authority of God onely, to bee that, wherein the bleſſing conſiſts, and that in ſuch wiſe alſo, as is nothing but a way of reproach, in the eyes of all the world, that a King ſhould ride into his chiefe City, ſo ſtrangely furniſhed, upon an Aſſe borrowed, her furniture old, overworn garments, and accompanied with none but poore, meane, excommunicated perſons, ſuch as your Elders, Scribes, Phariſees, Lawyers, and all your credible perſons among you,make full account they are not onely accurſed by, but alſo deſtitute and void of all law, when you can finde *Hoſanna* in the higheſt, ari-ſing out of ſuch contempt and ſhame, then, and then onely ſhall you ſing unto him with comfort.   In the meane time acknowledge your portion, which is to truſt and ſtay your ſelves on the name of man, and in his beautie to delight and glory, which ſhall fade as a leafe,and like the graſſe ſhall wither when it is fitting it ſelf for the oven, ſuch is man whoſe breath is in his noſtrills, and the ſonne of ſorrie man, in whom you delight to truſt, his power and his poli-cy brings forth nothing elſe, but as you ſhall ſee and heare in the Countrey from whence wee are brought.   We are not ignorant of thoſe ſhamefull lies and falſities gone out againſt us, and the daily wreſting of our words, to caſt contempt upon us, thinking to bow downe our backs under ignominie and reproach; Neither of thoſe ſtraits & difficulties they have caſt us upon, in the things which con-cerne this preſent life, to the taking away of the lives of many, if our God had not been ſeen beyond and above what their thoughts could reach unto (as their owne confeſſion hath witneſſed,) doing

it

it in such a way of painted hypocrisie and false glosse unto the eye of the world, that wee might seeme unto it self-executioners. We RESOLVE therefore to follow our imployments, and to carry and behave our selves as formerly wee have done(and no otherwise) for wee have wronged no man, unlesse with hard labour, to provide for our families, and suffering of grosse, idle, and idol droanes to take our labour out of the mouths, and from off the backs of our little ones, to lordane it over us.

So that if any any shall goe about to disturbe or annoy us henceforth in our imployments and liberties, which God hath, or shall put into our hands, that can claime no interest in us but by these courses; what their businesse is, wee know by proofe sufficient, to bee nothing else but that ancient errand of *Nimrod*, that rebellious hunter after the precious life; which errand of his shall bee no more delivered unto us in that covert cruelty, and dissembling way of hypocrisie, but in direct and open termes of tyrannie, wee will not bee dealt with as before, wee speake in the Name of our God, wee will not; For if any shall disturb us, as above, secret hypocrites shall become open Tyrants, and their lawes appeare to bee nothing else but meer lusts in the eyes of all the world.

And wherefore doe you murmure among your selves at this saying, thinking it is not a Christian expression? it is because you are ignorant of the crosse of our Lord Jesus, not knowing what it is: Therefore it is, that while you inveigh against such as set up a Statue of wood and stone, to bow downe unto it, and are so vaine, as to crosse the aire, (to use your owne expression) upon the face of infants, when they sprinkle them with water to as great purpose: And in the meane time you preach and set up *Seghnirim* for your crosse, whom you fall downe unto so willingly, and left you let the word passe without exposition of it unto all, it signifies, Horrour and feare, which is the crosse you hold and teach, and by and thorow which you thinke to bee saved, which is a name given by our Lord unto the Devill himself, as our English translate it, and the Lord never gives name, as an empty title, butaccording to the nature of the thing named; so that if hee speake, I have said yee are gods, of any besides himselfe, it is to declare, that there is not onely the name, but the very nature of the god of this world, and therefore hee saith, they shall die, even as *Adam*,which aspired and usurped the place of God, and fall also as one of the Princes, even

as

as one of thofe princes of *Midian,* whofe carkaffes became dung
for the earth; and hee that gives that title unto any but the true
God (that made heaven and earth) in any other fenfe but as it declares a flat oppofition againft God, is re-acting that ancient fpirit
of the ferpent, if yee eate, you fhall bee as gods, to judge of good
and evill, for which all men are fet up in that kinde; even fo,while
you tell the people, that by forrow, compunction, and anxiety,and
trouble of minde, they communicate in the fufferings of Chrift,
out of which condition their comfort is to flow, is nothing elfe
but to conclude the fonne of God to be Belial, yea, to affirme him
to bee *Seghnirim* himfelf; this doth hee receive at your hands in
your miniftries, for all your fawning upon him with a kiffe, fo
that if you will know how farre you are from communicating in
the death of Chrift, take it in this parable, verily, as farre as the
weaknefs of God is ftronger then man.

Country-men, for wee cannot but call you fo, though wee finde
your carriage towards us to bee fo farre worfe then thefe Indians,
wee advife you to take things together, and what God hath joyned, let none dare to put afunder: So that if you bee afhamed of
the croffe in Baptifme, bee afhamed of the Baptifme alfo, for fuch
as the croffe is, fuch is the Baptifme, therefore your anceftors goe
beyond you in that, to joyne croffing of the aire, and fprinkling
with the element of water together, but where ever Baptifme according to the word of Chrift is, there is the croffe of Chrift alfo,
they can no more bee feparated, then his fcepter and kingdom can,
for where the one is, there is the other alfo, and as they are co-
incident,fo are they co-apparant; So that if ever you fee the baptifme of Chrift truly in ufe, and exercifed upon any,you do as truly
fee that party partaking and communicating with the croffe and
fufferings of the Lord Jefus Chrift,.and to fee perfons in fuch eftate,
and to conclude that afterwards they may bee worthy of cenfure,
yea poffibly unto an *anathema maranatha,*is nothing elfe but to conclude a totall and finall falling away from the grace of God, as
your fathers have done before you; for no grace greater then the
croffe of our Lord Jefus.

Behold therefore you defpifers, the vanity and abomination of
all your baptifmes, how prejudiciall they are to the croffe of
Chrift: bee afhamed and return in time, or hee fhall bee a fwift witneffe againft you for ever, when your repentance fhall come too
late:

late; but you thinke the croffe of Chrift is not, but onely in bowing the back under every burden, and cringing and crouching unto
the luft of every man, otherwife his *Shebett* is not fit, nor fuiteth it
at all with your Regiment, unleffe fo fervile, that every man may
ferve his owne lufts of him, to get wealth and honour, friends and
allies, by fetting bounds and limits unto the holy Word of God;
fome in the way of one device, and fome according to another, and
he that will not either walk as a dumbe beaft, (worfe then *Balaams*
Affe) and fay nothing, or elfe give a fenfe of the holy writings
to maintaine the devifed platforme, if mercy muft bee ufed, not to
hang and burn, yet banifhment is ready waiting upon them; therefore fhall you know by the Rod of his power that comes out
of *Sion*, that hee will bee Ruler, even in the midft of his
enemies.

Per us whom you ftile your neighbours of *Providence,*you have
faid it, *Providence* is our Hold, the neighbourhood of the *Samari-
tan* wee profeffe.   And for the lookings on, and turnings afide of
your Priefts and Levites, without either unction, or bowells of
compaffion, all thofe flaine and wounded in foule amongft you,
finding no remedy, doe plainly teftifie unto all men the nature of
your travailes and neighbourhood what it is, that neither the
oyle of thofe two olive trees,nor the fatneffe of that vine , which
maketh glad God and man , is converfant amongft you; your
fpeech to us in generall, not ufing our names , whereas wee know,
it is particulars you aime at, gives us plainely to fee, the word
Ælem revived and living in you, as it ftands with its coherence in
Pfalme 58.

John Wickes
Randall Howldon
Robert Potter
Samuel Gorton
John Greene
Francis Wefton
Richard Carder
Richard Waterman
Nicholas Power
John Warner
William Waddell

From

From our Neck: Curo, September 15. 1643.

TO the great and honoured Idol Generall, now set up in the
Massachusets, whose pretended equity in distribution of Justice
unto the soules and bodies of men, is nothing else but a meer device
of man, according to the ancient customes & sleights of Satan, trans-
forming himself into an angel of Light, to subject and make slaves
of that species or kinde that God hath honoured with his owne
Image, read *Dan.* 3.Chap. wherein (if it be not like *Lots* love unto
the *Sodomites*) you may see, the visage or countenance of the State,
for wee know the sound of all the musick, from the highest note
of wind-instruments, sounding, or set up by the breath or voices
of men, (to have dominion and rule as though there were no God
in heaven or in earth but they, to doe right unto the sonnes of
men)unto the lowest tones of the stringed instruments, subjecting
themselves to hand or skill of the devised ministrations of men,
as though God had made man to bee a vassall to his owne species or
kinde, for hee may as well bee a slave to his belly, and make it his
God, as to any thing that man can bring forth, yea, even in his
best perfection, who can lay claime to no title or terme of honour
but what the dust, rottennesse, and putrefaction can affoord, for
that of right belongeth solely to our Lord Christ.   Woe therefore
unto the world, because of the Idols thereof; for Idols must needs
be set up, but woe unto them by whom they are erected.
     Out of the abovesaid principles, which is the kindome of dark-
nesse and of the devill; you have writ another Note unto us, to
adde to your former pride and folly, telling us againe, you have
taken *Pumham,* with others into your Jurisdiction and Government, and that upon good grounds (as you say:) you might have
done well to have proved your selfe Christians, before you had min-
gled your selves with the heathen, that so your children might
have knowne how to put a distinction betwixt yours and them in
after times, but wee perceive that to bee too hard a worke for your
selves to performe, even in time present.   But if you will communicate Justice and Government with that Indian, wee advise you to
keep him amongst your selves, where hee, and you may performe
that worthy worke: Yet upon a better ground, wee can informe
you that hee may not expect former curtesies from us, for now by
                                                              your

your Note, wee are refolved of his breach of Covenant with us, in
this his feeking and fubjeĉtion unto you, which formerly hee hath
alwayes denyed; let him and you know therefore, that hee is to
make other provifion for his planting of corne hereafter, than upon *Mfhawomet*, for wee will not harbour amongft us any fuch
fawning, lying, and cadaverous perfon as hee is, after knowledge
of him, as now in part you have given unto us, onely hee fhall have
liberty fufficient to take away his corne, habitation, or any of his
implements, fo be it hee paffe away in peace and quiet,which might
in no cafe bee admitted, if it were fo that wee lived by blood, as
you doe, either through incifion of the nofe, divifion of the eare
from the head, ftigmatize upon the back, fuffocation of the veines,
through extremity of cold, by your banifhments in the winter, or
ftrangled in the flefh with a halter.   But we know our courfe, profeffing the kingdome of God and his righteoufneffe, renouncing
that of darkneffe and the devill, wherein you delight to truft, for
without the practife of thefe things , you cannot kiffe your hand,
bleffe the Idol, nor profeffe your vowes and offerings to bee paid
and performed.   O yee generation of vipers, who hath fore-war-
ned you, or fore-ftalled your mindes with this, but Satan himfelfe,
that the practice of thefe things is to fly from the wrath to come;
Whereas the very exercife and performance of them, is nothing elfe
but the vengeance and wrath of God upon you already , in that
mankind, fo harmonically made in the Image of God , is in the
exercifes of the kingdome, become the torturer and tormentor, yea
the executioner of it felfe, whilft thofe of you that are of the fame
ftock and ftem, worke out, yea, and that curioufly, through the
law of your mindes, the death and deftruction of one another ;
when as, in the meane time, the fame nature or fubfiftance, in the
way of our Lord Jefus, faves both it felfe and others.   You tell
us of complaints made by the Indians, of unjuft dealings and injuries done unto them, why doe they not make them knowne to us,
they never complained to us of any thing done unto this day , but
they had fatisfaction to the full, according to their owne minde, for
oft wee know, in what they expreffe unto us, although our wrongs
infufferable done by them lie ftill in the deck, for wee know
very well, wee have plenty of caufeleffe adverfaries, wanting no
malice that Satan can inject, therefore wee fuffer much, that in the
perfection and heighth of their plots, they may receive the greater
rebuke

rebuke and fhame for their bafeneffe, in the eies of all the world.

To which end wee have not onely committed our condition unto writings, but them alfo into the hands and cuftody of fuch
friends, from whom they fhall not bee taken by any, or by all the
governments of this Country, as formerly they have beene, that fo
our wrongs might not appeare ; therefore never picke a quarrell
againft us in thefe things, for wee know all your ftiles and devices,
that being you now want fuch as old malicious *Arnauld,* one of
your low ftringed inftruments, to exercife his fidle amongft us, and
wee are void of your benediction alfo, fprung out of the fame ftock
to make rents and divifions for you to enter to gaine honour unto
your felves in having patients to heale, though they lie never fo
long under your hands, your chirurgerie muft bee thought never
the worfe. Wanting thefe or fuch like of the Englifh, to be-
tray the liberties, God hath given us into your hands, now you
worke by your coadjutors, thefe accurfed Indians ; but you are de-

[Errata: l. 17
& 18, read Cup
for Cope.]
ceived in us, we are not a Cope fitted for your fo eager appetite, no
otherwife, then if you take it downe it fhall prove unto you a Cope
of trembling, either making you vomit out your owne eternall
fhame, or elfe to burft in funder with your fellow confeffor for aire,

[Errata: l. 21,
read as Judas.]
Judas Ifcariot.

For Mr. *Winthrop* and his Copartner *Parker,* may not thinke to
lay our purchafed plantation to their Iland fo neere adjoyning,
for they come too late in that point, though *Benedick* hath reported that *Myantonimo,* one of the *Sachims,* of whom wee bought it,
fhould lofe his head for felling his right thereof to us.

As alfo a minifter affirmed that Mr. *Winthrop* fhould fay to him,
that wee fhould either bee fubjected unto you, or elfe removed
hence, though it fhould coft *Bloud.*   Know therefore, that our lives
are fet apart already for the cafe wee have in hand, fo wee will lofe
nothing but what is put apart aforehand, bethinke your felves
therefore what you fhould gaine by fetching of them, in cafe it were
in your power, for our loffe fhould bee nothing at all.

For wee are refolved, that according as you put forth your felves
towards us, fo fhall you finde us transformed to anfwer you.   If
you put forth your hand to us as country-men, ours are in readineffe for you: If you exercife the pen, accordingly doe wee become
a ready writer; If your fword bee drawne, ours is girt upon our
thigh; If you prefent a gun, make hafte to give the firft fire: for we
are

are come to put fire upon the earth, and it is our defire to have it
fpeedily kindled.

For your purfuite of us, ftill, to come your Courts, to receive
your parcells of Juftice, undoubtedly either God hath blinded your
eyes that you fee not our anfwer formerly given in that point, or
elfe you are moft audacious to urge it upon us againe; alfo you
may take notice that wee take it in more difdaine then you could
doe, in cafe we fhould importune you (yea) the chiefe amongft you,
to come up to us, and bee employed according to our pleafure, in
fuch workes as wee thought good to fet you about ; and for your
grant of freedome unto us to come downe to you, and returne in
fafety, wee cannot fufficiently vilifie this your verball and perfunctory offer, knowing very well, according to the verdict of your
owne confcience, that what wrongs foever are paffed amongft us
fince our comming into this Country, you have beene the violent
agents, and wee the patients.   To feare therefore to come amongft
you as fuch as have done wrong, the caufe vanifheth in us, fo muft the
effect alfo.   And to feare to come unto you as tyrants, which your
grant muft neceffarily implies, wee cannot, knowing that hee which
is with us, is ftronger then hee which is with you.

Alfo the earth is the Lords and the fullneffe thereof, and when,
and where hee fhall call wee will goe, but not at the will and luft of
forry men to play their parts with us at their pleafure, as formerly
they have done, and as it is apparant you defire to doe, for if your
lufts prevailed not over you in that kinde, you might well thinke
that wee have better employments then to trot to the *Maffachufets*
upon the report of a lying Indian, or Englifh either, as your factors
and ordinary hacknies doe.

But know this O yee——that fo long as wee behave our felves as
men, *walking in the name of our God,* where ever wee have occafion
to come, if any mortall man whofe breath is in his noftrils, dares to
call us into queftion, wee dare to give an anfwer to him, or them,
nor fhall wee faile through God, to give teftimony even in his confcience of the hope that is in us, whether his queftion may concerne
the rice or fucceffion either of Prieft or Peere.   In the meanetime
we fit in fafety under the cloudy pillar, while the Nations roare
and make a noife about us, and though you may looke upon us
with the unopened eye of *Eliahs* fervant, thinking us as nothing to
thofe that are againft us, yet wherever the cloud refts, wee know the
Lords

Lords returne to the many thousands of Israel.

[Errata: l. 3, leave out to.]

In that you say our freedome granted to come to you, takes a-way all excuse from us, wee freely retort it upon your selves to to make excuses, whose Lawes and proceedings with the soules and bodies of men, is nothing else but a continued art (like the horse in the mill) of accusing and excusing, which you doe by circumstances and conjectures, as all the fathers have done before you, the Diviners and Necromancers of the world, who are gone to their owne place and have their reward; But for the true nature, rise, and distribution of things as they are indeed and shall remaine and abide as a law firme and stable forever, wee say and can make it good, you know nothing at all, therefore such as can delight themselves in preaching, professing, and executing of such things, as must end as the brute beasts doe, nay take them away for present and they have lost their honour, religion, as also their God ; let such wee say, know themselves to bee that beast and false prophet, no man of God at all.   In the meane time wee looke not on the things that are seene, but on the things that are not seene, knowing the one are temporary, the other eternall.   Nor doe wee thinke the better of any man for being invested into places or things that will in time waxe old as doth a garment, neither judge we the worse of any man for the want of them: for if we should we must condemne the Lord Christ, as so many doe at this day.

Wee demand when wee may expect some of you to come to us, to answer and give satisfaction for some of these foule and inhu-mane wrongs you have done, not to the Indians, but to us your country-men: not to bring in a Catalogue, as we might, take this one particular abuse you are now acting; in that you abet, and backe these base Indians to abuse us.   Indeed *Pumham* is an aspiring person, as becomes a Prince of his profession, for having crept into one of our neighbours houses, in the absence of the people, and felloniously rifled the same, hee was taken comming out againe at the Chimney-top: *Soccononoco* also hath entred in like manner into one of our houses with divers of his companions, and breaking open a chest, did steale out divers parcels of goods, some part whereof, as some of his companions have affirmed, are in his custody at this time. Yet we stand still to see to what good issue you will bring your proceedings with these persons, by whom you are so honorably attended in the Court generall, as you call it, and would ho-

nour

nour us alſo, to come three or foureſcore miles to ſtand by you and
them ; wee could tell you alſo that it is nothing with theſe fellowes
to ſend our cattle out of the woods with arrowes in their ſides, as
at this preſent it appeares in one even now ſo come home, and it is
well they come home at all, for ſometimes their wigwams can receive them, and wee have nothing of them at all; yea they can do-
mineere over our wives and children in our houſes, when wee are
abroad about our neceſſary occaſions, ſometimes throwing ſtones,
to the endangering of their lives, and ſometimes violently taking
our goods, making us to runne for it if wee will have it, and if wee
ſpeake to them to amend their manners, they can preſently vaunt
it out, that the *Maſſachuſets* is all one with them, let the Villanie
they doe bee what it will , they thinke themſelves ſecure, for they
looke to bee upheld by you in whatever they doe, if you bee ſtronger
then them which they have to deale withall, and they looke with
the ſame eye your ſelves doe, thinking the multitude will beare
downe all, and perſwade themſelves (as well as they may) that you
tolerate and maintaine them in other of their daily practices, as lying, Sabbath-breaking, taking of many wives, groſſe whoredomes,
and fornications, ſo you will doe alſo, in their ſtealing, abuſing of
our Children, and the like, for you have your diligent ledgers
amongſt them that inculcate daily upon this, how hatefull wee are
unto you, calling us by other names of their owne deviſing, bearing them in hand, wee are not Engliſh men, and therefore the object of envy of all that are about us, and that if wee have any thing
to doe with you, the very naming our perſons.ſhall caſt our caſe bee
it what it will, as it is too evident by the caſe depending betweene
William Arnauld and *John Warner*, that no ſooner was the name of
Mr. *Gorton* mentioned amongſt you, but Mr. *Dudley* diſdainefully
asking,is this one,joyned to *Gorton*, and Mr.*Winthrop* unjuſtly upon the ſame ſpeech, refuſed the oath of the witneſſe calling him
knight of the poſt : are theſe the wayes and perſons you trade by
towards us? are theſe the people you honour your ſelves withall?the
Lord ſhall lay ſuch honour in the duſt, and bow downe your backes
with ſhame and ſorrow to the grave, and declare ſuch to bee Apo-
ſtatiſers from the truth, and falſifiers of the word of God onely to
pleaſe men,and ſerve their owne luſts, that can give thankes in their
publique Congregations for their unity with ſuch groſſe abominations as theſe. Wee muſt needes aske you another queſtion from
a Ser-

a Sermon now preached amongſt you, namely how that bloud re-
liſheth you have ſucked formerly from us, by caſting us upon
ſtraights above our ſtrength, that, have not beene exerciſed in
ſuch kinde of labours, no more then the beſt of you in former times
in removing us from our former conveniences, to the taking away
of the lives of ſome of us, when you are about your diſhed up dainties, having turned the juice of a poore ſilly Grape that periſheth in
the uſe of it, into the bloud of our Lord Jeſus by the cunning skill
of your Magicians, which doth make mad and drunke ſo many in
the world,and yet a little ſleepe makes them their owne men againe,
ſo can it heale and pacifie the conſciences at preſent, but the leaſt
hand of God returnes the feares and terrour againe, let our bloud
wee ſay preſent it ſelfe together herewith, you hypocrites when
will you anſwer ſuch caſes as theſe, and wee doe hereby promiſe unto you, that wee will never looke man in the face if you have not a
fairer hearing then ever wee had amongſt you, or can ever expect;
And bee it knowne to you all, that weeare your owne Country-
men, whatever you report ofus, though the Lord hath taught us a
language you never ſpoake, neither can you heare it,and that is the
cauſeof your alienationfrom us;for as you have mouthes and ſpeake
not,ſo have you eares & heare not;ſo we leave you to the judgement
andarraignment of God Almighty. *The joynt act,not of the Court Generall, but of the peculiar fellowſhip, now abiding upon Mſhawomet*
                                                    Randall Holden.
This they owned in Court though onely Holdens *hand were to it.*

Poſtſcriptum.

VV EE need not put a ſeale unto this our warrant, no more
        then you did to yours. The Lord hath added one to our
hands, in the very concluſion of it, in that effuſion of bloud, and
horrible Maſſacre, now made at the Dutch plantation, of our loving Country-men, women, and children, which is nothing elſe,
but the compleate figure in a ſhort epitomie of what wee have writ,
ſummed up in one entire act, and left you ſhould make it part of
your juſtification,as you do all ſuch like acts, provided they bee not
upon your owne backes, concluding them to be greater ſinners then
your ſelves, wee tell you (nay) but except you repent, you ſhall
likewiſe periſh.

                                                            For

For wee aske you who was the cauſe of Miſtreſſe *Hutchinſon* her departure from amongſt you, was it voluntarie? No, ſhee changed her phrafes according to the dictates of your tutors, and confeſſed her miſtakes, that ſo ſhee might give you content to abide amongſt you, yet did you expell her and caſt her away ; no leſſe are you the originall of her removall from *Aquethneck*, for when ſhee ſaw her children could not come downe amongſt you, no not to conferre with you in your own way of brotherhood;but be clapt up,and detained by ſo long impriſonment, rumors alſo being noiſed, that the Iſland ſhould bee brought under your Government, which if it ſhould, ſhee was fearefull of their lives, or elſe to act againſt the plaine verdict of their owne conſcience, having had ſo great and apparant proofe of your dealings before, as alſo the Iſland being at ſuch diviſions within it ſelfe, ſome earneſtly deſiring it ſhould bee delivered into your hands, profeſſing their unity with you, others denyed it, profeſſing their diſſent and diviſion from you, though for what themſelves know not, but onely their abominable pride to exerciſe the like tyranny.

From theſe and ſuch like workings having their originall in you, ſhee gathered unto her ſelfe and tooke up this fiction, (with the reſt of her friends) that the Dutch plantation was the Citie of refuge, as ſhee had gathered like things from your doctrines before, when ſhe ſeemed to hold out ſome certaine glimpſes or glances of light, more then appeared elſewhere whilſt there was ſuch to approve it, in whom there might bee ſome hope to exalt the inſtruments thereof, higher then could bee expected from others, but you know very well you could never reſt nor bee at quiet, till you had put it under a Buſhell, *id eſt*, bounded and meaſured the infinite and immenſe word of God, according to your owne ſhallow, humane, and carnall capacities, which, howſoever may get the higheſt ſeates in your Synagogues,Synods, and Jewiſh Synedrions, yet ſhall it never enter into the kingdome of God to be a doorekeeper there. Do not therefore beguile your ſelves in crying out againſt the errours of thoſe ſo miſerably falne, for they are no other things which they held but branches of theſame rootyour ſelves ſo ſtoutly ſtand upon,but know thiſthat now the axe is laid to the root of the tree, whereof you are a part, and every tree that brings not forth fruit according to the law of that good things, which the father knowes, how to give to thoſe that aske it, ſhall bee cut
downe

downe, and caſt it into the fire : Neither doe you fill up your
ſpeeches or tales , (wee meane your Sermons) but that wee affect
not the Idolizing of words , no more then of perſons or places.
For your ſelves know the word is no more but a bruit or talke, as
you know alſo your great and terrible word Magiſtrate, is no more
in its originall, then Maſterly, or Maſterleſſe, which hath no great
luſtre in our ordinary acceptation.   Therefore wee looke to finde
and injoy the ſubſtance , and let the ceremony of theſe things ,
like vapours vaniſh away , though they gather themſelves into clouds, without any water at all in them,the Lord is in the mean
time a dew unto *Iſrael,* and makes him to grow like a lillie, caſting
out his roots and branches as *Lebanon.*

We ſay, fill not up your talk as your manner is, crying, that ſhee
went out without ordinances , for God can raiſe up out of that
ſtone, which you have already rejected,as children, ſo alſo miniſters
and ordinances unto *Abraham*: You may remember alſo, that
every people and poore plantation, formerly fleeced by you, cannot reach unto the hire of one of your Levites , nor fetch in , one
ſuch Dove as you ſend abroad into our native Country,to carry and
bring you news.

Nor can you charge them in that point,for it was for protection
or government ſhee went; And however, hire, in other reſpects,
yet the price of a wife, and ſafetie of his owne life adjoyned, carryed a Miniſter along with them of the ſame riſe and breeding together with your owne, to adde unto the blood ſo ſavagely and cauſe-
leſly ſpilt, with a company of ſuch as you take pleaſure to protect,
for they are all of one ſpirit , if they have not hands in the ſame
act; we ſay their death is cauſeleſſe, for wee have heard them affirm
that ſhee would never heave up a hand , no nor move a tongue a-
gainſt any that perſecuted or troubled them, but onely indeavour
to ſave themſelves by flight, not perceiving the nature and end of
perſecution, neither of that antichriſtian oppoſition and tyrannie,
the iſſue whereof declares it ſelf in this ſo   and lamentable.

Note, good Reader, that I had order to publiſh theſe two
Letters of his, as well *literatim* as *verbatim,* but becauſe their Or-
thography was ſo bad, as it would ſcarce have been underſtood, I
left it to bee corrected by the Printer, but no word to be changed:
And the reaſon of the word here left out, is, becauſe it was worne
and

out, and ſo ſoyled in the originall as wee could not read it , and thought good rather to leave it a blanck, then to put in a word of our own that was not theirs.

In the next place, I preſent thee here with certaine Obſervations collected out of both their Letters, by a godly and reverend Divine, whereby the Reader may the better underſtand them , and indeed try the ſpirits of theſe men, whether they be of God or no. Now theſe his Obſervations are ranked into three Heads: *Viz.*

Firſt, their reproachfull and reviling ſpeeches of the Government and Magiſtrates of the *Maffachuſets*, which in *Gortons* Booke hee pretends ſo much to honour, becauſe their Government is derived from the State of *England*; and therefore I deſire thee to take the better notice of it.

The ſecond Head of his Obſervations directs thee to their reviling language, not onely againſt that particular Government , and the Magiſtrates of it, but againſt Magiſtracy it ſelfe, and all Civill power.

And in his third Head, thou art directed to take notice of their blaſphemous ſpeeches againſt the holy things of God. All which becauſe they are of great concernment, I beſeech the Reader to take a little paines to compare them with Mr. *Gortons* and his Companies Letters.

Certaine

Certaine Obfervations collected out of both their *LETTERS*.

I. *Their reproachfull and reviling Speeches of the Government and Magiftrates of the Maffachufets.*

Pag. 9.

1. Hey fay our Magiftrates did lay their Wifdome pro-ftrate, in fending Letters to them, which they fcornfully call an irregular Note.

2 That they bare them caufleffe enmity, the proofe whereof every occafion brings forth.

3 They flily call them the feed of the ancient mother; *i.* of the enmity of the Devill.

4 That they know it is the name of Chrift call'd upon them, a-gainft which our Magiftrates doe ftrive.

5 That they goe about to hide their fin, as *Adam*, bearing the world in hand, that they defire not to contend, but to redreffe fome-thing in point of Civill peace.

6 That they ftand on tip-toe to ftretch themfelves beyond their bounds, to feek occafion againft them.

7 That thofe who accufe them, are accufers of the Brethren, Sa-tan being a lyer, and the father of it; which thing our Magiftrates cannot know though they be told of it.

Pag. 10.

8 That this act of theirs to treat about their land, is a mappe of their fpirituall eftate.

9 That they delight daily to eate of the forbidden fruit (which they call mans wifdome) out of which our Churches and Com-mon-wealth is formed) to gaine conformity with their maker.

10 They fcorn at their purity and godlineffe, telling them that *Cole* and *Arnold* their diffembling fubjects, are full of the fpirit of their purity.

11 They doe not fay plainly that our Magiftrates are dogs, but compare them to dogs in refuming their vomit into its former

con-

concoction, by receiving *Cole* and *Arnold* under our jurifdiction.

12 That the whole ftructure and edifice among us (*i.* the Churches and Common-wealth) is raifed up in the fpirit of an hireling, and that by fubmiffion to the Word of God in fafting, feaftfting, retiredneffe for ftudy, contributing, treafuring (*i.* for Church ufes in feverall Churches) they doe nothing elfe but bring forth fruit unto death.

13 That farther then the Lord Jefus agrees with riches, honour and eafe, our Magiftrates minde him not, nay, renounce, and reject him.

14 That they plainely crucifie Chrift, and put him to an open fhame, which the Apoftle, *Hebr. 6.* applies to the worft of men, who commit the unpardonable fin, and for whom men are not to pray. *Pag.* 11.

15 That our Magiftrates are as farre from yeelding fubjection to Chrift, as *Cole* and *Arnold* from being honourable and loyall fubjects, whom they call the fhame of Religion, the difturbance and difquiet of the place, diffembling fubjects, *pag.* 10. as alfo deboift, rude, inhumane *Nabals*, il-bred, apoftatifed perfons, and fellonious, *page* 23. with many fuch like fpeeches. *Pag.* 12.

16 That the things of Gods kingdome are infinitely beyond the reach of their fpirit, nor can they heare the lively Oracle, and therefore are dumb in telling Juftice.

17 That the Magiftrates are Jewes according to the flefh, and ftout maintainers of the man of Sin.

18 That they know our Magiftrates eyes are dazled with envy, and their ears open to lyes. *Pag.* 13.

19 That they judge them before their caufe be heard. *Pag.* 15.

20 That in inviting them to their Courts for their equal-ballanced Juftice (as they fcornfully call it) they thereby ftrike at Chrift their life.

21 That our Magiftrates are like *Herod,* whom God fmote with wormes, for feeking by an out-reaching and circumventing policy to fubdue *Tyrus* and *Sidon,* and like *Pontius Pilate,* and the people who out of the Judgement hall are all for mercy, but in it nothing but crucifie him, crucifie him, bee their accufations, and witneffes never fo falfe, fo (fay they) in your dealings with men in way of the Jewifh brotherhood, your law is all for mercy, to redreffe, reforme, for prefervation of foule and body, doe but enter into the Com- *Pag.* 16.

Common-hall, then if witneffes bee but brought in, and oath taken though never fo untrue, your Confciences are purged by law , and your power muft have tribute paid it,fo far as to brand mens names with infamy, and deprive women and children of things neceffary.

22 That the profeffed clemency and mercy of their law, is as much as in them lyes, to fend both foule and body downe to *She-ol* (*i.* the grave and hell) forever, without redreffe and all hope of recovery.

23 That their houre and power of darkneffe is knowne, what it is either to have mens perfons in admiration becaufe of advan-tage, or elfe to feek all occafions againft them, with all manner of reproach and ignominie.

Pag. 17.   24 That their wayes are wicked, and to bee abhorred, becaufe in their profeffed courfe the two witneffes are flaine by them, and put to death; and that all their glory is to keep their corpfe unbu-ried; and thefe two witneffes are the life and death of the Lord Jefus.

Pag. 18.   25 That the light appearing among them, is nothing but the light of *Balaam*, fo that in feeing, they fee not, but communicate onely in the light of that Beaft who put the witneffes to death.

26 They tell our Magiftrates , that they never come amongft them, but they fee themfelves in a regiment of groffe and palpable darkneffe,and difcern you to fcrabble on the wall for the door of *Lots* houfe.

Pag. 19.   27 That they know not what a true witneffe is.
*Pag.*22, 23.   28 That the whole Word of God is a parable to them, as their converfation in all points daily declare it.

29 That they will not come neare our Magiftrates, untill they know they beare another minde from their neighbours, whom they call robbers, groffe diffembling hypocrites, who doe nothing but goe about to eftablifh fuch wayes as may maintaine their owne vicious lufts, whofe laws are pretended and devifed, and whofe pra-ctifes(they fay)they renounce as diabolicall.

Pag. 24.   30 Yee blind guides(fay they to our Magiftrates)as your fathers have ever done, fo do you.

Pag. 25.   31 You fet up *Segnirim* (*i.* as themfelves interpret) feare and horrour, or the devill, by, and for the which you hope to bee faved.

Pag. 26.   32 That their carriage towards them, is farre worfe then that of
the

the *Indians,* whom themſelves cry out of to bee thieves and robbers; *pag.*32.

33 That they are deſpiſers; Behold(ſay they) yee deſpiſers, the vanity and abominations of all your baptiſmes.

34 Yee think (ſay they) that the croſſe of Chriſt is nothing but bowing down the back to every burden, and cringing and crouching to the luſt of every man.

35 They call the generall Court, the great Idol Generall, whoſe *Pag.* 28. pretended equity in diſtributing Juſtice is a meer device of man according to the ſleights of Satan.

36 They tell the Court, that out of the kingdome of darkneſſe and the devill, they had writ another Note to adde to their former pride and folly.

37 For taking *Pumham* and *Sachanonoco (Indian Sachims)* under their protection; they tell the Court they might have done well to have proved themſelves Chriſtians before they had mixt themſelves with the heathen; but this was too hard for them to doe.

38 They adviſe the Court(in ſcorn)to keep the *Indian* with them, *Pag.* 29. where he and they might perform that worthy work of diſtributing Juſtice.

39 They tell the Court that they live by bloud.

40 They tell the Court,they renounce the kingdom of darkneſs, and the devill, wherein the Court delights to truſt.

41 They call the Court, O ye generation of Vipers.

42 They tell the Court, they are not a cup fit for their appetite, *Pag.* 30, 31. but a cup of trembling either to make them vomit up their owne eternall ſhame, or elſe to make them burſt aſunder with their fellow confeſſor *Judas Iſcariot.*

43 That the Court is either blind or audacious in deſiring them to come for their parcells of Juſtice, and that they diſdain to come to them.

44 They profeſſe they cannot ſufficiently vilifie the promiſe of theCourt, that they ſhall come down to them and return in ſafety; which they call a verball and perfunctory offer.

45 They tell the Court, that if their luſts had not prevailed over them, they might thinke they had better employment then to trot to *Maſſachuſets* as their factors, and ordinary hackneys doe.

46 They tell the Court that their lawes and proceedings with *Pag.* 32.
the

the foules and bodies of men, is nothing elfe but a continued act
of accufing and excufing (like the horfe in the mill) which (fay
they) you doe by circumftances and conjectures, as alfo your fathers have done before you, the Diviners and Necromancers of
this world, who are gone to their owne place, and have their reward.

Pag. 33.   47 They accufe our Magiftrates for maintaining *Indians* in
their lying, fabbath-breaking, groffe whoredomes, ftealing, &c.

Pag. 34.   48 That they are hypocrites, having eyes and fee not, eares and
hear not, mouths and fpeak not.

Now had thefe men returned a rationall anfwer, it might have
been meet perhaps by a few marginall Notes to have returned fome
fhort Reply; but both their Letters being fraught with little elfe
then meer raylings, and reproachfull language, it may be fufficient
thus to prefent them in one view together, that fo the wife and prudent may take a tafte of their fpirits, and learne from what fire it
is that their tongues are thus highly inflamed. If our Courts and
Magiftrates had been in any thing to blame, what a faire and eafie
way had it been to have firft convinced them, before they had thus
bitterly reviled them; but thus to cut and fhave, and caft all this
filth in their faces without proof or reafon, argues a bold and infolent fpirit fitted to make combuftions and confufions in the place
where they live. If indeed the Magiftrates had given them any fore
provocations of returning ill language, there might have been fome
excufe , but alaffe, all the caufe that can bee given of moft of this
ill language, is nothing but writing friendly unto them, to fend
fome from themfelves to clear up the differences between them and
the *Indians* , and to fhew their juft title to the land they poffeffed:
if they had kept this flood within their owne bankes , or been but
moderate in revilings, it might have been winkt at ; but to fly out
into fuch extremity on fo fmall provocation againft their betters,
fo as to call them Idolls, blind-guides, defpifers, generation of vipers, fuch as crucifie Chrift, men that ferve their owne lufts, hypocrites, the feed of the Devill, Necromancers, Judaffes, men that
live by bloud, robbers and thieves, men without mercy, among
whom Juftice is dumbe, delighting in the kingdome of darkneffe
and the devill, like *Herod* and *Pilate* in adminiftring Juftice, whofe
eyes are dazled with envie, and eares open to lies, ftout maintainers
                                                                    of

of the man of Sin, whofe wayes are wicked, and to bee abhorred; worfe then *Indians*, like dogs, &c. This language fpeakes loud to what Countrey they belong,and of what race they come.

I I. *Their reviling Language not onely againft the Magi- ftrates and Government here in particular,but alfo againft Magiftracy it felf, and all Civill power.*

IF any fhall fay for them (as themfelves now for their owne ad- vantage doe) that this ill language is directed onely againft our particular Government and Magiftrates, but not againft all Civill power it felf, the contrary may appear (notwithftanding their dark language, under which fome times they feek to conceale it) in thefe particulars.

"1 They exprefly affirm that the Office to minifter Juftice, be- *Pag.* 16.
"longs onely to the Lord : and that therefore(from their inftance
"of *Herod*) men make themfelves Gods, (which themfelves inter-
"pret to be onely from the God of this world, and to be in flat op-
"pofition againft God, *pag.* 26.) by ruling over the bodies and e-
"ftates of men;and that the people receiving *Herod* toGovernment,
"& crying out that this was the ordinance of God,and not of man,
"that he was immediately fmitten of God for it: As alfo they tell
"us, *p.* 26.that to fet up men to Judge of good and evil, for which
"all men are fet up in that kinde ; that this is re-acting that
"ancient fpirit of the Serpent, If yee eate, yee fhall bee as
"Gods.

Now this ftrikes at all Magiftracy, for if the office of miniftring juftice and righteoufneffe belongs to God onely,then not unto any man, for that is to make Gods of men; and if to judge betweene good and evill bee to act over againe the ancient fpirit of the Ser- pent, then 'tis not onely unlawfull, but diabolicall, to make Jud- ges of what is right and wrong, good or evill by any man.

If it bee objected, is it poffible that any men fhould bee fo grofly blind and wicked, as to abolifh all miniftration of Juftice and righ- teoufneffe?

Anfw. 1. Thefe men feeme to acknowledge fome way of mini- ftring Juftice, but the myfterie lies in that word *Office*, they would
have

have no man ſet up in the Office of Magiſtracy, diſtinguiſhed from
other men, but would have ſuch a power common to the Brethren, ſo that a man may judge as a brother, but not as an Officer,
and therefore they ſlily juſtifie him, who called one of our chiefe
Magiſtrates in the open face of the Court, *Brother*, and condemne
all our Magiſtrates, becauſe every man doth not ſit there to judge as
a Brother, *pag.* 16. and their reaſon ſeems to bee drawne from this,
becauſe that to bee a Brother, and conſequently a coheire with
" Chriſt, is a higher ſphere then to bee a Civill Officer, as their
owne words intimate, *pag.* 16. Now the rule is evident *à quatenus
ad omne,* that if miniſtration of Juſtice and judgement belongs to
no officer, but to a man as a Brother, then to every Brother, and if
to every Brother, whether rich or poore, ignorant or learned, then
every Chriſtian in a Common-wealth muſt bee King, and Judge,
and Sheriffe, and Captaine, and Parliament man, and Ruler, and
that not onely in *New-England,* but in *Old,* and not onely in *Old,* but
in all the Chriſtian world; downe with all Officers from their
Rule, and ſet up every Brother for to Rule, which the godly-wiſe
may eaſily diſcerne to bee the eſtabliſhment of all confuſion,
and the ſetting up of Anarchy worſe then the greateſt Tyranny.

2. Although theſe may beare the world in hand that they allow
miniſtration of Juſtice and righteouſneſſe by men as Brethren, yet
ſome Cakes of theſe mens dough have been ſo farre leavened and
ſowred againſt all Civill power, as that in our Publike Courts, being demanded how murderers, theeves, and adulterers ſhould bee
puniſhed if there ſhould bee no Civill power coercive, they openly
and roundly anſwered before many witneſſes, that ſuch perſons
muſt be left to the judgment of God, both which not long after God
himſelf ſate Judge upon, being ſuddenly and barbarouſly ſlaine by
the bloody *Indians* in the *Dutch* plantation.

Pag. 18, 19.   " Firſt, they exclaime againſt us for chooſing men that are ho-
" nourable, learned, wiſe, experienced, and of good report, or
" elſe they may not rule among us, and this, they ſay, is of man,
" and by man, and putting the ſecond witneſſe to death, *viz.* the
" death or weakneſſe of Chriſt, or in plaine Engliſh, 'tis a killing
" of Chriſt.

Now however the application is made unto our Civill State, yet
it manifeſtly ſtrikes at all Civill States in the world, who ſhall
chooſe

chooſe any Officers for rule and government, and adminiſtring of Juſtice, although they bee never ſo honourable, learned, wiſe, experienced, and of good report, and conſequently moſt fit for government; and that in ſo chuſing them they doe put Chriſt himſelf to death.   So that theſe men ſtill harp on that ſtring to have every man judge as a Brother, whether honourable or not honourable, whether wiſe or fooliſh, whether of good report or evill report, otherwiſe Chriſts weakneſſe is ſlaine.

   3. " They affirme that they who can create, make void, and   *Pag.* 22.
" remove offices and officers at their pleaſure, are of that evill one,
" (*i.* the devill) and not of Jeſus Chriſt, but of *Shedim* that waſter
" and deſtroyer of mankind for ever.   Their proofe is from that monſtrous interpretation of Yea, yea, and Nay, nay, and they inſtance not onely in Church-officers, but in Common-wealth-officers, whether Rulers or Captaines.   Their words are theſe,
" *viz.* Hee with whom it is yea, I am a Ruler, but it was nay when
" I was none at all, renounceth the ſpirit of him that rules in righ-
" teouſneſſe, profeſſing the ſpirit of him that is Prince of the
" power of the aire, who is working now ſo effectually in the
" children of diſobedience; ſo alſo hee with whom it is yea, I
" am captaine, or chief-ſlaughter-man, but it was nay, time was
" that I was none at all, renounceth the victory and ſlaughter
" made by the Captaine and High-prieſt of our profeſſion,
" profeſſing himſelfe to bee a ſuperfluous Giant made in the
" hoſt of the *Philiſtims,* to defie the hoſt of the living God.

   By which ſpeeches 'tis evident that they doe not onely oppoſe Civill officers choſen amongſt us here, but all ſuch as are choſen Rulers, Captaines, and Officers at any time, in any place, and were not ſo before; and ſuch they ſay are of the Devill the deſtroyer of man.

   4 " They ſay men limit, and ſo deſtroy the holy one of *Iſrael,*   *Pag.* 18.
" whoſe life is infinite, and without circumſcription and contain-
" ment (as they call it) if men acknowledge that Chriſt rules on
" earth onely by his Deputies, Litvtenants, and Vicegerents, (*i.* by
" perſons inveſted with Civill authority and office, for ſo they
are called by Orthodox Divines) and therefore they ſay that his
" putting Chriſt to death, when onely wiſe, and honourable, and
" learned, and experienced, and men of good report, are choſen
" to rule, becauſe they would have the *Power* to rule common to
                                      all

all Chriſtians, but as for the *office* of rule to bee peculiar to none,
"and therefore *Pag.* 24. they tell us that none ſhall ſee Chriſt come
"into his kingdome with comfort, untill the authority and pow-
"er of man appeares to be as the building of *Babel,* and the name and
"authority of God onely to bee that ,wherein the bleſſing conſiſts;
meaning that 'tis Babyloniſh building which God miſliked, and con-
founded, for any man in office to rule and governe, becauſe this is
to limit the power and life of Chriſt (which is in every brother
as well as in any officer) and ſo to kill the life of Chriſt; ſo that if a-
ny of them ſay that although they diſtaſte officers, as Kings and o-
thers by election, yet not ſuch as are ſo by hereditary ſucceſſion,
they are but words to ſute their owne ends for a time, and to delude
others,for if it bee limiting the holy One of Iſrael, a circumſcribing
and ſo deſtroying the life of Chriſt which is infinite, for to make
him rule by his Deputies and Vicegerents on earth, then not onely
Kings and Princes, whether by election or no, but all other civill
officers muſt bee abandoned, becauſe the life and power of Chriſt is
limited in ſucceſſive as well as in elective Princes, in inferiour as
well as in ſuperiour governours, who are Chriſts Deputies, and
Vicegerents, and therefore called *Rom.* 13. 4. the Miniſters of God
either for good or terrour.

Pág. 28.   5. They call our generall Court the Idoll generall, which is no-
"thing elſe but a device of man by the ſleight of Sathan to ſubject
"and make ſlaves of that ſpecies or kinde which God hath hono-
"red with his owne Image , and they do not onely ſpeake thus
"of our Courts as Idols, but they cry out woe unto the world be-
"cauſe of the Idols thereof, for Idols muſt needes bee ſet up, but
"woe be unto them by whom they are erected, and their reaſon
"reacheth to all civill power,(for ſay they) a man may be as well a
"ſlave to his belly,and make that his god,as be a vaſſall to his owne
"ſpecies, or kinde, or to any thing that man can bring forth even in
"his beſt perfection.

There are other evidences of thèir corrupt minde herein from o-
ther paſſages in their letters which they ſpeake under more obſcure
cloudes and allegories,but theſe may bee a ſufficient witneſſe againſt
them before men and angels, that they abandon all civill authority,
although for to ſerve their owne turnes of others or their owne
luſts, they ſay they do not: the Apoſtle *Jude* long ſince, tels us of
ſuch perſons expreſly who deſpiſe Dominion and ſpeake evill of
                                                    Dignities

Dignities, 1. They doe not only deſpiſe theſe or thoſe particular perſons or ſtates that are inveſted with Dominion; but they deſpiſe Dominion it ſelfe and Dignities themſelves, and would have all that power abandoned, whom he calleth *v*:8.filthy dreamers, defiling the fleſh, murmurers and complainers walking after their owne luſts, their mouthes ſpeaking great ſwelling words, *v.* 16. And that it may yet more fully appeare that theſe men doe abandon all civill authority, (although this ſecret they will not impart unto all, but rather profeſſe the contrary) there is extant to bee ſhewen if need were, the writings betweene a prudent man in this Country, and one of the chiefe, and moſt underſtanding of this peculiar fellowſhip (as they ſtile themſelves) wherein hee doth ſtoutly maintaine theſe three aſſertions, 1. That there are no Ordinances. 2. That there are no relations neither in the Common-wealth betweene rulers and ſubjects, nor in the Church between officers and brethren, nor in the families betweene husband and wife, maſter and ſervant, father and ſonne. 3. That there are no inherent graces in Chriſtians. By which principles the world may ſee what theſe men goe about, *viz.* as much as in them lies to bring in a diſorder and confuſion in all ſtates and families, and to open the ſluce to all violence, injuſtice, and wickedneſſe, by not only abandoning, but reproaching and revi-
"lingall civill rule and authority upon earth, which they therefore
"ſcornefully call a meere device of man, Idols, to be of the Devill,
"the deſtroyer of mankinde, and to bee a crucifying of Chriſt in
"his life and death, and all this when honourable, wiſe, learned,
experienced, well reported perſons are choſen and inveſted with Civill power, whom therefore they would not have maintained, and to whom it is as unlawfull to adminiſter any oath for the ending of civill differences, as to luſt after a woman to commit adultery, *Pag.* 20.

III.　*Their　blaſphemous　ſpeeches　againſt　the　holy　things　of
　　　God.*

1. **A**Gainſt the Churches, they call them deviſed platformes *Pag.* 26.
"*Pag.* 26. and that the wiſedome of men is the whole ac-
"compliſhment(or that which gives the whole being) of Churches and Common-wealth. *Pag.* 10.　　　　　　　　2. "Againſt

*Pag.*11.   2. "Againft the calling of Minifters, they fay,that to make their
"calling mediate and not immediate, is to make a nullity of Chrift,
"and to crucifie Chrift, and to put him to an open fhame, and that
"fuch Minifters are Magicians, *Pag.* 34.

Now this reflects upon all the Ordinances and ordinary Officers
and Minifters of Chrift, that either are or have beene in the
Church at any time, for although the offices bee immediately
from Chrift, yet their call to éxercife this office hath beene ever
accounted mediate.

Pag. 36.   3. "Againft the word of God, they call the Sermons of Gods
"Minifters *tales*, or *lies* and *falfhoods*, now had they thus fpoken upon proofe againft any particular Sermons, or perfons, the accufed might have fpoken for themfelves, but indifferently to revile all
Sermons as tales or forgeries, the doctrine generally taught here a-
mongft us, being no other then that which *Paul* preached at *Ephe-
fus* for three yeares fpace and upwards, *viz.* repentance towards
God,and faith towards the Lord Jefus, *Act.* 20. being alfo no o-
ther then what agrees generally with the harmony of confeffions
of all reformed Churches: to call thefe tales is a word which the
Lord Jefus will certainely remember, unleffe they repent; the Sermons of the Apoftles of Chrift, as well as the doctrine of all reformed Churches, being reproached hereby.

Pag. 26.   4. Againft the Sacraments: as for baptifme they doe not onely
make the baptizing of Infants as abominable as the croffe, but all
our baptifmes, "behold (fay they) the vanity and abomination of
all your baptifmes, and they doe not meane all thofe baptifmes
which are in ufe amongft us, but in any Churches of the world at
this day; for they acknowledge no other baptifme then that which
is fpirituall, and hence they fay, "that when ever you fee the bap-
"tifme of Chrift truly in ufe according to the word of God, you
"doe as truly fee that party partaking and communicating with
"the croffe and fufferings of Chrift, for thefe are coaparant, now
communicating in Chrifts fufferings in their meaning is onely fpirituall,and fo is therefore all baptifmes. 2. As for the Lords fupper
fcarce a greater heape of blafphemies in fewer words can come from
the mouth of man againft that bleffed Ordinance, wherein Chrift is
fo manifeftly and fweetly prefent, "for they call it your difht up
"dainties, turning the juice of a fillie grape that perifheth in the ufe
"of it,into the bloud of the Lord Jefus, by the cunning skill of
                                                            "your

"your Magicians, which doth make mad and drunke fo many in
"the world.

5. Againft repentance and humiliation for finne, they fpeake
fomewhat obfcurely, but they that know them may foone underftand their meaning, which if it be this, that in a way of compunction and forrow for finne, a Chriftian is not to feeke for confolation and comfort from Chrift, and to affirme that this is to
make the fonne of God *Belial* and *Segnirim*, the Devill himfelfe, (as
they interpret it) then tis moft groffe blafphemy againft not onely
the preaching, but practife of repentance and godly forrow, for
which the Apoftle rejoiced to fee in the Corinthians, *ch.* 7 *v.*9.10.
and which *James* and *Peter* command and commend, *James* 4. *v.* 9.
10. 1 *Peter* 5. *v.* 6. and which way not fo much *Mofes* in the law
but Chrift in the Gofpell hath fanctified to finde pardon of finne
1 *John* 1. 9.

6. Againft Chrift Jefus himfelfe: "they condemne our doctrine
"for affirming that Jefus Chrift actually dyed and fuffered onely in
"the dayes of *Herod,* and *Pontius Pilate,* when hee hanged on the
"Croffe, and that hee was crucified in truth and fubftance onely
"when hee appeared borne of the Virgin *Mary*: and for this do-
"ctrine wee are condemned as Wifards and Necromancers.

Now what is this but to overthrow not onely the being of Chrift
in the flefh, making him no other then fuch an one as actually fuffered from the beginning of the world, and fhall doe to the end of it,
but alfo overthrowing all faith and hope of falvation in that Meffiah who was incarnate in the dayes of *Herod* and *Pilate,* and in his
death and fufferings, and that one perfect offering, then once for all
*Heb.*10.14. The reader may therefore be pleafed to take notice that
being asked in open Court what was that Chrift who was borne
of the Virgin and fuffered under *Pilate?* one of them anfwered that
hee was a femblance, picture, or a fhadow of what was and is done
"actually and fubftantially in Chriftians ; and hence the meaning
of the words may bee gathered *Pag.* 11. which otherwife the wife
reader may thinke to bee non-fence. *viz.* "that they are Wifards
"and Necromancers who raife a fhadow without a fubftance (*viz.*
"to make Chrift to bee flaine in types fince the worldbegan) or
"who raife the fubftance of him who dwels in light without a fha-
"dow, (making no more of Chrift but a femblance and fhadow, as
themfelves call it) for further explication of which they affirmed
in

Pag. 26.
Ex 1. *pag.*
They fay out
of the forbid-
den fruite i. e.
mans wifdom,
our Churches
and Common-
wealth is for-
med. 2. That
the whole edi-
fice amongft
us is raifed up
in the fpirit of
an hireling. 3.
That by fub-
miffion to the
word of God
in fafting,feaft-
ing, retired-
neffe for ftudy,
contributing,
treafuring, i. e.
for Church u-
fes fo much in
feverall Chur-
ches, they doe
nothing but
bring forth
fruite unto
death.

Pag. 11.

in open Court that as the Image of God in *Adam* was Chrift, ("for "God they faid had but one Image) fo the loffe of this Image by "man was the death of Chrift, and therefore'tis no wonder if they deny Chrift to dye actually onely when crucified under *Pontius Pilate* becaufe man finned actually (which they make to be Chrifts death) long before; meane while the reader may take notice with a holy aftonifhment and horrour of the heavy curfe of God in blinding thefe bold men with fnch a palpable and groffe fpirit of delufion and mad phrenfies, who will make mans finne and fall, which is the caufe of perdition ofmen, to be the caufe of theSalvation of man, for fo Chrifts death is which they blafphemoufly make mans finne to bee.

For further proofe that they make little ufe of Chrift and his death, then as hath been faid, their owne interpretation of the flaying of the two witneffes, *Pag.* 17. 18. feemeth to confirme, for they make thefe two witneffes the life and the death of Chrift in men, the life of Chrift they call his ftrength, and the death of Chrift they call his weakneffe, *viz.* as it is, and appeares in weake, foolifh, ignorant, unexperienced, and ill-reported of men, and therefore they blameus for killing of Chrifts death (for it feemes it is fuch a death as may bee killed) in that wee chufe honourable, wife, learned men, and of good report to place of rule, excluding others.

Now fome of thefe blafphemies might have beene the better borne if they had let Chrift and his death alone, and his word alone, but to call the holy word and Sermons of Salvation *tales*, the Sacrament an abomination, madding and making drunke the world, to call the Minifters of Chrift who difpenfe Word and Sacraments, Necromancers and Magicians, and they who hold and beleive him to bee the Meffiah and Chrift who fuffered under *Pilate*, Wifards, and all this in coole bloud, in the open face of the Court, obftinately refufing to alter a title of what they had writ, let the world judge if ever Antichrift that beaft fpoken of *Rev.* 13. 5, 6. did ever fpeake greater blafphemies againft God, his name, and tabernacle, and whether fuch men deferve to live, that live thus to blafpheme; may not fuch civillftates that tolerate fuch, feare that fentence of Godagainftthem as was pronounced againft *Ahab* for letting blafphemous *Benhadab* efcape with his life, *thy life for his life*? however mens charity may enlarge it felfe this way, yet let wifedome preferve us and make the wifehearted wary of fuch impoftors, who want not their wiles to fay

and

and unſay, as may beſt ſute their advantage,for they can hold forth at ſome time and to ſome perſons, wholeſome and orthodox truths and beare them in hand that this is all that they hold,but they have depths of abomination to give to drinke when theyſee their ſeaſons, in ſuchgolden cups;they have hidden ſecrets,which their youngProſelytes ſhall not preſently ſee, much leſſe others; for ſo they tell us *Pag.* 17. "that tis not their purpoſe to open to every one the houſe "of their treaſures, the ſilver and gold, and ſpices, and precious "ointment, nor the houſe of their armour, becauſe they may take "them all as execrable and put them to a prophane uſe, nor can "every ſpirit comprehend the breadth of the land of *Emanuel,* (as "they call it *Pag.*12.) nor know the Cherubims of glory, nor the "voice of the oracle from the Mercy-ſeate: and indeed their uncouth, tumorous and ſwelling words (as *Jude* cals them *Jude* 16). like ſwellings, and tumours of the fleſh, arethe undoubted ſignes of a ſecret and ſeducing humour, whereby they are fit to deceive the ſimple and infect the ſtrong, if men bee not watchfull.

The Publiſher to the Reader.

THE reaſon wherefore nothing is anſwered to the great charge in his voluminous Poſtcript, is becauſe it hath beene anſwered already by a former treatiſe printed: but more eſpecially becauſe many of the friends, children and kindred of the dead are in good eſteeme with us, whom I am loath to grieve.

But ſince by courſe thou art next to caſt thine eye Gentle Reader upon the ſumme of a Preſentment which the Court at *Road Iland* received from theirGrandJewry being preſent when *SamuelGorton* had ſo much abuſed their Government in the face of the Country,yea in open Court, their owne eyes and eares bearing witneſſe thereunto, they I ſay preſented theſe abuſes to the Court, as ſuch which they conceived ought not to bee borne without ruine to their Government, and therefore beſought the bench to thinke offome one puniſhment for examples ſake as well as otherwiſeto bee inflicted on the Delinquent.

And therefore that thou maiſt ſee the occaſion thereof, take notice that an ancient woman having a Cow going in the field where
Samuel

Samuel Gorton had fome land. This woman fetching out her Cow,
Gortons fervant maid fell violently upon the woman beating and notorioufly abufing her by tearing her haire about her, whereupon
the old woman complaining to the Deputy Governour of the place,
hee fendeth for the maid, and upon hearing the caufe, bound her
over to the Court. The time being come and the Court fet, *Gorton* appeares himfelfe in the defence of his maid, and would not fuffer his maid to appeare or make anfwer, but faid exprefly fhe fhould
not appeare, and that if they had any thing againft her they fhould
proceed with him. And though hee was lovingly diffwaded by
fome of the Bench not to engage himfelfe but let his maid appeare,
yet hee refufed: but when hee could not bee prevailed with, the
action was called and witneffes produced, fworne, and examined:
which being done, hee moved for another witneffe to bee called,
which hee perfwaded himfelfe and the Bench was an honeft woman and would fpeake the truth. Now fhee being fworne, faid,
Mr.*Gorton*, I can fpeake nothing will helpe your maid. And indeed
her whole teftimony was againft her and for the old womans caufe,
whereupon hee openly faid, Take heed thou wicked woman, the
earth doth not open and fwallow thee up. And then hee demanded of the Court if hee fhould have equity and juftice in his caufe or
no? To which was anfwered, if he had either plea or evidence to
produce in his maids caufe it fhould be heard. Then hee nomina-
ted one *Weekes* who could fay fomething to it. *Weekes* was called
and required to take his oath before hee fpake; at which *Gorton*
and *Weekes* both of them jeered and laughed and told the Court they
were skilled in Idols, and that was one, and ftood ftoutly a long time
to make it good. Hereupon fome of the Court put him in mind how
they had forewarned him of fuch carriages fearing he would fall into fome extreames. At length the Governour gathering up the
fumme of what was witneffed, commends it to the Jewry. At which
time *Gorton* faid, the Court had perverted Juftice and wrefted the
witneffes, with very many high and reproachfull termes; and in
the midft of his violence throwing his hands about, hee touched the
Deputy Governour with his handkerchiefe buttons about his
eares (who it feemes fate at a Table with his backe towards him)
whereupon the Deputy faid, what will you fall about my eares? To
which *Gorton* anfwered I know not whether you have any eares or
no? and if you have, I know not where they ftand; but I will not
touch

touch them with a paire of Tongues. The Governour often calling upon the Jewry to attend the Caufe, was as often interrupted
by him. Whereupon many of their Freemen being prefent, defired the Court they would not fuffer fuch infolencies,profeffing they
were troubled the Court had borne with them fo long. For which
in briefe, hee was committed, but when the Governour bade the
Marfhall take him away ; hee bade take away *Coddington*, which
was their Governours name: a thing I thought meet to explaine,left
thou fhouldft not underftand it by the Heads of the Prefentment
here following, abufing all and every particular of the Magiftrates
with opprobrious terms. But note when hee was committed upon
his mutinous and feditious fpeeches, *Weekes, Holden, &c.* his abet-
tors, ftopped the way with fuch infolency, as the Governour was
forced to rife from the Bench, to helpe forward the Command
with his perfon, in clearing the way, put *Weekes* in the ftocks, and
was forced to command a guard of armed men to preferve themfelves and the peace of the place: And this they did becaufe of
fome fore-going jealoufies; and now taking occafion to fearch the
houfes of that party that adhered to him, they found many of
their peeces laden with bullet: and by meanes hereof they were forced to continue their guard,whilft upon their banifhment they were
forced from the Ifland.

And however it were enough for a Book alone to relate all the
particulars of his infolent carriage, yet take notice onely of two
or three particulars: 1 When hee was cenfured to bee whipt and
banifhed, he appealed to *England*; they asked to whom? Hee faid
with a loud voice, *To King Charles*. They told him, hee fhould
firft have his punifhment, and then afterwards hee might complain.
To which hee replyed, take notice *I appeale to King Charles, Celo,*
or *Selah*; the party who was prefent told mee hee could not tell
which , but that word was fpoken with an extraordinary high
and loud voice.

A fecond thing to be obferved, was , that after hee had been fo
defervedly whipt, fome of his faction faid, Now Chrift Jefus had
fuffered.

And thirdly, although the weather was very cold,the Governour
going away after execution of Juftice upon him, yet he ran a good
way after the Governour, drawing a chaine after one of his legs,
the upper part of his body being ftill naked, and told him, He had
but

but lent him this, and hee should surely have it again. All this I
had from a man of very good repute, who then lived with them,
and was an eye and eare witnesse to all these proceedings.

In the next place take notice good Reader, that when hee went
from hence well whipt, as before, and entred upon his banishment,
the place hee went to (in a sharpe season) was a Town called *Providence,*where Mr. *Roger Williams,*& divers others lived,who in regard
of the season, entertained them with much humane curtesie, but
the *Gortonians* answered all like *Æsops* snake, as thou maist read
by the severall Letters of the chief Inhabitants of that place, by
a notorious faction there also by them raised, to the great distracti-
on and amazement of the Inhabitants, as appeareth by their dole-
full complaints in their own Letters, a true Copy whereof I present
unto thee.

[Errata: l. 10,
for by read in.]

The sum of the Presentment of Samuel Gorton *at* Portsmouth *in* Roade-Island, *by the Grand Jury.*

First, that *Samuel Gorton* certaine dayes before his appearance at
this Court, said, the Government was such as was not to bee
subjected unto,forasmuch as it had not a true derivation, becaufe it
was altered from what it first was.

2 That *Samuel Gorton* contumeliously reproached the Magistrates
calling them Just Asses.

3 That the said *Gorton* reproachfully called the Judges, or some
of the Justices on the Bench (corrupt Judges)in open Court.

4 That the said *Gorton* questioned the Court for making him
to waite on them two dayes formerly, and that now hee would
know whether hee should bee tryed in an hostile way, or by Law,
or in sobriety.

5 The said *Gorton* alledged in open Court, that hee looked at
the Magistrates as Lawyers, and called Mr. *Easton*, Lawyer
Easton.

6 The said *Gorton* charged the Deputy Governour to bee an
Abetter of a Riot, Assault, or Battery, and professed that he would
not touch him, no not with a paire of tongues: Moreover he said,
I know not whether thou hast any eares,or no: as also,I think thou
knowest

knoweft not where thy ears ftand, and charged him to be a man unfit to make a Warrant.

7 The faid *Gorton* charged the Bench for wrefting witneffe, in
this expreffion,I profeffe you wreft witneffe.

8 The faid *Gorton* called a Freeman in open Court (faucy Boy,
and Jack-an-Apes;) and faid, the woman that was upon her oath,
would not fpeake againft her mother, although fhe were damned
where fhe ftood.

9 The faid *Gorton* affirmed that Mr. *Eafton* behaved himfelfe not
like a Judge,and that himfelf was charged either bafely or falfly.

10 The faid *Gorton* faid to the Bench, Ye intrude Oaths,and goe
about to catch me.

11 The faid *Gorton* being reproved for his mifcarriage, held up
his hand, and with extremity of fpeech fhooke his hand at them,
infomuch that the Freemen prefent faid, Hee threatens the Court.

12 The faid *Gorton* charged the Court with acting the fecond
part of *Plymouth* Magiftrates, who, as hee faid, condemned him in
the Chimney corner,ere they heard him fpeak.

13 The faid *Gorton* in open Court did profeffe to maintaine the
quarrell of another being his Maid-fervant.

14 The faid *Gorton* being commanded to prifon, imperioufly
refifted the authority, and made open Proclamation, faying, take a-
way *Coddington*, and carry him to prifon; the Governour faid again,
all you that owne the King,take away *Gorton* and carry him to prifon; *Gorton* replyed,all you that own the King,take away *Coddington*, and carry him to prifon.

William Dyre Secretary.

Mr. Roger VVilliams *his Letter unto Mr.* VVinthrop,
concerning Samuel Gorton.

Providence 8. 1ᶠᵗ. 1640.

MAfter *Gorton* having foully abufed high and low at *Aquednick*,
is now bewitching and bemadding poore *Providence*, both
with his uncleane and foule cenfures of all the Minifters of this
Country,(for which my felf have in Chrifts name withftood him)
and alfo denying all vifible and externall Ordinances in depth of
Familifme,

Familifme, againſt which I have a little diſputed and written, and ſhall (the moſt High affiſting) to death: As *Paul* ſaid of *Aſia*, I of *Providence* (almoſt) All ſuck in his poyſon, as at firſt they did at *Aquednick*.   Some few and my ſelfe withſtand his Inhabitation, and Towne-priviledges, without confeſſion and reformation of his uncivill and inhumane practiſes at *Portſmouth :* Yet the tyde is too ſtrong againſt us, and I feare (if the framer of Hearts helpe not)it will force mee to little Patience, a little Iſle next to your Prudence.   Jehovah himſelfe bee pleaſed to bee a Sanctuary to all whoſe hearts are perfect with him; In him I deſire unfainedly to be

> *Your Worſhips true and affectionate*

> Roger Williams.

Providence this **17.** *of November, Anno* **1641.**

To the Honoured Governour of Maſſachuſett, together with the Worſhipfull Affiſtants, and our loving Neighbours there.

VVEe the Inhabitants of the Town aboveſaid, having faire occaſions, counted it meet and neceſſary to give you true intelligence of the inſolent and riotous carriages of *Samuel Gorton* and his company, which came from the Iſland of *Aquednick*; which continue ſtill as ſojourners amongſt us; together with *John Greene,* and *Francis Weſton,* two which have this long time ſtood in oppoſition againſt us, and againſt the faireſt and moſt juſt and honeſt ways of proceedings in order and Government, that wee could rightly and truly uſe, for the peaceable preſervation and quiet ſubſiſtence of our ſelves and families, or any that ſhould have faire occaſion to goe out or come in amongſt us.   Alſo ſix or ſeven of our Townſmen which were in peaceable Covenants with us, which now by their declamations doe cut themſelves off from us, and jointly under their hands have openly proclaimed, to take party with the afore-named Companies, and ſo intend for ought wee can gather, to have no manner of honeſt order, or government either over them or amongſt them, as their writings, words, and
actions

actions doe moſt plainly ſhew. It would bee tedious to relate the numberleſſe number of their upbraiding taunts, aſſaults, and threats, and violent kinde of carriage daily practiſed againſt all that either with care or counſell ſeek to prevent or withſtand their lewd licentious courſes. Yet in briefe to commit ſome few of them to your moderate Judgements, leſt wee our ſelves ſhould bee deemed ſome way blinded in the occurrences of things, here is a true Copy of their Writing incloſed, which *Francis Weſton* gave us the 13. of this preſent Moneth, they having alſo ſetup a Copy of the ſame on a tree in the ſtreet, in ſtead of ſatisfaction for fifteene pounds, which by way of arbitration of eight men orderly choſen, and all cauſes and reaſons that could bee found, daily and truly examined, and conſidered jointly together, when hee the ſaid *Francis Weſton* was found liable to pay, or make ſatisfaction in Cattle or Commodities, but on the 15. of this preſent moneth, when wee went orderly, openly, and in a warrantable way to attach ſome of the ſaid *Francis Weſtons* Cattle, to drive them to the Pound, to make him, if it were poſſible, to make ſatisfaction: which *Samuel Gorton* and his company getting notice of, came and quarrelled with us in the ſtreet, and made a tumultuons Hubbub; and although for our parts wee had before-hand moſt principally armed our ſelves with patience, peaceably to ſuffer as much injury, as could poſſibly bee born, to avoid all ſhedding of blood, yet ſome few drops of blood were ſhed on either ſide: And after the tumult was partly appeaſed, and that we went on orderly into the Corne-field, to drive the ſaid Cattle, the ſaid *Francis Weſton* came furiouſly running with a flayle in his hand, and cryed out, Helpe Sirs, helpe ſirs, they are going to ſteale my cattle, and ſo continued crying till *Randall Holden*, *John Greene*, and ſome others came running and made a great outcry, and hollowing and crying, Theeves, theeves, ſtealing cattle, ſtealing cattle, and ſo the whole number of their deſperate company came riotouſly running, and ſo with much ſtriving in driving, hurried away the cattle, and then preſumptuouſly anſwered, they had made a reſcue, and that ſuch ſhould bee their practiſe if any men at any time, in any caſe attach any thing that is theirs. And fully to relate the leaſt part of their ſuch like words and actions, the time and paper would ſcarce bee profitably ſpent, neither need wee to adviſe your diſcretions what is likely to bee the ſad events of theſe diſorders, if their bloody currents bee not either ſtopped, or turned fome other way. For it is plaine to us, that if men fhould continue to refift all manner of order, and orderly anfwering one of another in different cafes, they will fuddenly practife, not onely cunningly to detaine things one from another, but, o-penly in publike, juftly or unjuftly, according to their own wills diforderly take what they can come by; firft pleading neceffity, or to maintaine wife and family; but afterwards boldly to maintain licentious luft, like favage brute beafts, they will put no manner of difference between houfes, goods, lands, wives, lives, blood, nor any thing will bee precious in their eyes: If it may therefore pleafe you of gentle curtefie, and for the prefervation of humanity and mankinde, to confider our condition, and lend us a neighbour-like helping hand, and fend us fuch affiftance (our neceffity urging us to bee troublefome unto you) to helpe us to bring them to fatisfaction,and eafe us of our burden of them, at your difcretions; wee fhall evermore owne it as a deed of great charity, and take it very thankfully,and diligently labour in the beft meafure wee can, and conftantly practife to requite your loving kindneffe, if you fhould have occafion to command us, or any of us in any lawfull defigne: And if it fhall pleafe you to fend us any fpeedy anfwer,we fhall take it very kindly, and bee ready and willing to fatisfie the Meffengers, and ever remaine

Your loving Neighbours,and refpective Friends

Jofhuah Winfor
Benedict Arnold
William Mean
William Hawkings
Robert Weft

William Field
William Harris
William Wickenden
William Reinolds
Thomas Harris
Tho. Hopkins mark
Hugh Bennit
William Carpenter.

Providence

Providence the 25. of the 3. month, 1641.

To the reſt of the five Men appointed to manage the affaires of our Towne aforeſaid, Theſe are further to give you to un-derſtand; VIZ. That

I Doe not onely approve of what my neighbours before me have written and directed their Reaſons   to a ſerious conſideration with us, concerning *Samuel Gorton* and his Company: but this much I ſay alſo, that it is evident and may eaſily bee proved, that the ſaid *Samuel Gorton* nor his Company are not fit perſons to bee received in, and made members of ſuch a body, in ſo weake a ſtate as our Town is in at preſent.

My Reaſons are, *Viz.*

Firſt, *Samuel Gorton* having ſhewed himſelfe a railing and turbulent perſon, not onely in and againſt thoſe ſtates of Government from whence hee came, as is to bee proved; but alſo here in this Towne ſince hee have ſojourned here; Witneſſe his proud challenge, and his upbraiding accuſations in his vilifying and opprobrious terms of, and againſt one of our Combination moſt wrathfully and ſhameleſſly reviling him, and diſturbing of him, and medling with him, who was imployed and buſied in other private occaſions, having no juſt cauſe ſo to revile and abuſe him, ſaying alſo to him (and that of another ſtate) in a baſe manner, they were like ſwine that held out their Noſe to ſuck his blood, and that now hee and the reſt of his Company would goe and wallow in it alſo; which are indeed words unſufferable; and alſo deſpitefully calling him Boy, as though hee would have challenged the field of him, in ſuch an inhumane behaviour as becomes not a man that ſhould bee thought to be fit by any reaſonable men to be received into ſuch a poor weak ſtate as we are in at preſent.

Secondly, another of his Company, one who is much in eſteem with him, who openly in a ſcornfull and deriding manner, ſeeing one of the five men that was choſen by the Towne, and betruſted in the Towne affaires, comming towards him in the ſtreet, hee asked of one that ſtood by him, who that was; the other anſwered him, it was one of the five men appointed for managing of our Towne affaires,

affaires, or the like: Yea, faid hee, Hee lookes like one of
the five, which words import not onely a fcorning and deriding of his perfon ofwhom then hee fpake,but alfo a defpifing and
fcorning of our Civill State, as it were trampling it under foot,
as they had done by other States before they came hither, who
were of greater ftrength then wee are ; for which caufe I cannot
fee fuch perfons to bee fit to bee received into fuch a State as our
Towne is.

Thirdly, I cannot finde thefe men to bee reafonable men in their
fuite unto the Towne, to be received in as Townfmen, feeing they
have already had a plaine denyall of their requeft, and that by the
confent of the major part of the Towne, or very neare, &c. and
are yet unanfwerable ; and alfo that they feeing that their comming to our Towne, hath brought the Towne into a hurry,
almoft the one halfe againft the other, in which eftate no Towne or
City can well ftand or fubfift ; which declareth plainly unto us,
that their intent is not good, but that their abode fo long here a-
mongft us, is in hope to get the victory over one part of the Town,
but fpecially of thofe that laid the firft foundation of the place, and
bought it even almoft with the loffe of their lives, and their whole
eftates, and afterwards to trample them under their feet, as fome
of their words hold forth, or elfe to drive them out into the fame
condition, to feek out a new *Providence*, and to buy it with the like
hardneffe as they firft bought this place; thefe, and many other
like reafons that may be fhewed,declare that they are not fit perfons
to be received into our meane and weake State.

Fourthly, and feeing hee who is fo well knowne to bee the
ring-leader unto the breach of peace, that have been fo notoriofly
evill to bee a trouble of Civill States where hee hath lived, that are
of farre greater force then wee are of, fpecially that State who have
their Commiffion and Authority from the Higher Powers; what
may wee then expect if he could get himfelf in with, and amongft fo
many as wee fee are daily ready to tread us under their feet, and
his,whom he cals friends,&c.Surely,firft a breach of our civill peace,
and next a ruine of all fuch as are not of his fide, as their daily practife doth declare ; *Ergo*, they are not fit perfons to be received into
our Towne, &c.

Object. If it bee objected, as fome have blafphemoufly faid,
that wee are perfecutors, and doe perfecute the Saints, in not

receiving

receiving of them into our Towne-fellowſhip, &c.

Anſw. To this I anſwer, there cannot bee proved the leaſt ſhew of any perſecution of thoſe perſons, either by us, or by any other amongſt us to our knowledge. For 1 they have quiet abode a-mongſt us, none moleſting or troubling of them, nor any thing they have. 2 It cannot bee proved but by their owne relation, the which hath been diſproved; that they were ſent out from thoſe places from whence they came for Religion, neither are they med-led with here for any ſuch matter, but rather that they themſelves in their bravery are more ready to meddle with others. 3 They themſelves and others of their followers, have rather been trou-blers and perſecutors of the Saints of God that lived here before they came, and doe but waite their opportunity to make them-ſelves manifeſt in that they intend; *Ergo*, it cannot bee truly ſaid of any, that any perſecution is offered by us unto them, if it could poſ-ſibly be ſaid of them that they are Saints.

Obj. But if it be further objected, that we doe not give them the liberty of men, neither doe wee afford them the bowells of mer-cy, to give them the meanes of livelihood amongſt us, as ſome have ſaid.

Anſw. To this I ſay; 1 there is no State but in the firſt place will ſeeke to preſerve its owne ſafety and peace. 2 Wee cannot give land to any perſon by vertue of our combination , except wee firſt receive them into our ſtate of combination , the which wee cannot doe with them for our owne and others peace-ſake, &c. 3 Where-as their neceſſity have been ſo much pleaded, it is not knowne that ever they ſought to finde out a place where they might accommo-date themſelves, and live by themſelves, with their friends, and ſuch as will follow after them, where they may uſe their liberty to live without order or controule, and not to trouble us, that have taken the ſame courſe as wee have done for our ſafety and peace, which they doe not approve nor like of, but rather like beaſts in the ſhape of men to doe what they ſhall thinke fit in their owne eyes , and will not bee governed by any State. And ſeeing they doe but here linger out the time in hope to get the day to make up their penny-worths in advantage upon us, we have juſt cauſe to heare the com-plaints of ſo many of our Neighbors that live in the Town orderly amongſt us, and have brought in their complaints, with many rea-ſons againſt them, and not to admit them, but anſwer them as unfit

perſons

perfons to bee received into our meane State, &c.

Now if thefe Reafons and much more which have been truly faid of them, doe not fatisfie you, and the reft of our neighbours, but that they muft be received into our Towne-ftate, even unto our utter overthrow, &c. then according to the order agreed upon by the Towne, I doe firft offer my houfe and land within the liberty of the Towne unto the Towne to buy it of mee, or elfe I may, and fhall take liberty to fell it to whom I may for mine advantage, &c.

William Arnold.

A PARTICVLAR ANSWER

TO THE

Manifold Slanders and abominable Falfehoods

contained in a Book, called *Simplicities defence againſt
Seven-headed Policy:* Wherein *Samuel Gorton*
is proved a difturber of Civill Societies,defpe-
rately dangerous to his Country-men
the Englifh in *New-Engl.* and
notorioufly flanderous in what
he hath Printed of them.

HEN firft I entertained the defires of the
Countrey to come over to anfwer the com-
plaints of *Samuel Gorton,* &c. and to render a
reafon of the juft and righteous proceedings of
the Countrey of *New-Engl.* in the feverall parts
of it, againft him being a common difturber of
the peace of all Societies where hee came, witnes
New-Plymouth, 2 *Roade-Ifland,* 3 *Providence,* and laftly the *Maſſa-* — Sam. Gorton a
chuſets, being the moft eminent; I little thought then to have ap- common diftur
peared in print: but comming into *England,* and finding a Booke ber of the Civil
written by Mr. *Gorton* called *Simplicities defence againſt Seven-headed* peace in all the
policy: or, A true complaint of a peaceable people, being part of the Englifh there lived in.
in New-Engl. *made unto the State of Old-*England, *againſt cruell per-*
fecutors united in Church-Government in thoſe parts. I then conceived my felfe bound in duty to take off the many groffe and publike
fcandalls held forth therein, to the great amazement of many tender confciences in the Kingdom, who are not acquainted with his
proud

proud and turbulent carriage, nor fee the Lion under his Lambe-
skinne coate of *fimplicity and peace*. The Lord knowes how unwil-
ling I was perfonally to engage: and I truft hee will alfo guide mee
in anfwering his booke, as I fhall bee farre from bitterneffe: tis
true, time was when his perfon was precious in mine eies, and
therefore I hope and defire onely to make a righteous and juft defence to the many unworthy things by him boldly, ignorantly,
proudly, and falfly publifhed to the great difhonour of God in
wronging and fcandalizing his Churches, which the Lord Jefus
Chrift will not leave unpunifhed.

I know theworld is full of controverfies and tis my great griefe to
fee my dearnative Country fo engaged in them,efpecially one godly perfon againft another.   'Tis my prefent comfort I come not to
accufe any ; but to defend *New-England* againft the injurious complaints of *Samuel Gorton, &c.* but as it comes to paffe oftentimes
that men wound others unavoidably in defending their perfons
from the violent affaults of fuch as draw upon them, which otherwife they would never have done: fo if Mr. *Gorton* receive any
fuch hurt (which is unavoidable) hee becomes an acceffary thereunto: by forcing mee to defend the Country, without which I
fhould beeunfaithfull.

I know the world is too full of bookes of this kinde, and therefore however I am unfitted of many things I have and could procure at home would well become a relation of the late and prefent
ftate of *New England*, yet I fhall now onely with as great brevity as
may bee give anfwer to fuch injurious complaints as hee maketh
of.us.   And however his Title, Preface, and every leafe of his booke
may bee juftly found fault with, I fhall clearly anfwer to matters
of fact, fuch as hee chargeth the feverall Governments withall,fo as
any indifferent Reader may eafily difcerne how grofly wee are a-
bufed, and how juft and righteous cenfures were againft him for di-
fturbing the civill peace of all focieties where hee came, in fuch a
manner as no Government could poffibly beare: and for the *blafphemies* for which hee was proceeded againft at *Maffachufets*, they
fell in occafionally by his owne meanes withoutany circumftance
leading thereunto.

Pag. I.   And firft whereas hee accufeth us in the firft page of his booke to
goe over to *fuppreffe hereticks*. 'Tis well knowne we went thither
for no fuch end laid downe by us, but to enjoy thofe liberties the
                                                                    Lord

Lord Jefus Chrift had left unto his Church to avoid the Epifcopall
tyranny, and the heavy burthens they impofed,to which fufferings
the kingdome by this ever to bee honoured Parliament have and
doe beare witneffe to, as religious and juft.   And that wee might
alfo hold forth that truth and ancient way of God wherein wee
walke, which Mr. *Gorton* cals herefie.   Next in the fame *Pag.* hee
chargeth us with *affection of Titles, &c.* To which I anfwer,either we
muft live without Government, or if wee have Governours wee muft
give them wee call fuch Titles as are futable to their offices and places they beare in Church and Common-wealth, as Governours and
Affiftants, Paftors, Teachers, Rulers, Deacons,&c. thefe are our
higheft Titles we give.

In his fecond *pag.* hee chargeth the *Maffachufets to unite with other*   **Pag. 2**
*Colonies to the end they might bathe themfelves in bloud and feed themfelves
fat with the lives of their brethren, &c.*   This is a notorious flander.
'Tis true that the *Maffachufets* new *Plimouth, Conectacut,* and *New-
haven,* I meane the feverall Colonies there entred into a civill combination, and are called by the name of the *United Colonies,*and this
was occafioned by a generall confpiracy of the Indians againft the
body of the Englifh there feated,together with the diftracted condition of *England,*from whom we could expect no helpe at that time.
But Mr. *Gorton* and his company fell at that time into more then
ordinary familiarity with the *Nanohigganfet Indians,*who were the
principal contrivers of the Villany; who where they could not
draw others to them by force or flattery , they did it by large
gifts, &c. as I could prove by many teftimonies of the Indians, many hundred miles afunder from each other, in which defigne had
not the finger of God in much mercy prevented, I had beene the firft
had fallen; which I forbeare to relate here,being what I now doe, is
but an anfwer to his invective,

Next in the fame *pag.* hee tels us at his landing *how hee found his
Country men at great variance at Bofton in point of Religion;* But had
not hee holpen to blow the bellowes the flame might never have
beene fo great.   And whereas hee faid that *Mr. Williams was banifhed thence for differing from us being a man of good report,&c.* In anfwer,
1. take notice,I know that Mr. *Williams* (though a man lovely in his
carriage, and whom I truft the Lord will yet recall) held forth
in thofe times *the unlawfulneffe of our Letters Patents* from the King,
&c. would not allow the *Colours of our Nation,* denyed the *lawful-
neffe*

*neffe of a publique oath as being needleffe to the Saints, and a prophana-
tion of Gods name to tender it to the wicked, &c.* And truly I never heard
but he was dealt with for thefe and fuch like points: however I am
forry for the love I beare to him and his, I am forced to mention it,
but God cals mee at this time to take off thefe afperfions.

In *pag.*3. hee mentions the proceedings of the *Maffachufets* againft
Mr. *John Wheelwright &c.* Had it beene the will of God I would
thofe differences had never been: But the maine difference was about
a Petition by way of Remonftrance, which the Government tooke
very offenfive: But Mr. *Wheelwright* and they are reconciled, hee
having given fatisfaction, &c. In the fame *pag.* hee wrongs the doctrine of our Churches, which is well knowne to bee found.   But
whereas hee tels us in the fame *pag.* of denying *cohabitation, and
of whippings, confinement, imprifonment, chaines, fines, banifhment.* I
confeffe all thefe things befell him, and moft juftly: for hee was
bound to the good behaviour at *Plimouth* and brooke his bonds in
the face of the Court, whipt and banifhed at *Roade Ifland* for mu-
tinie and fedition in the open Court there: alfo at *Providence* as
factious there though his party grew greater then Mr. *Williams* his
better party, as appeares by his and their fad letters to the Government of the *Maffachufet* for helpe and advice ; and afterwards banifhed the *Maffachufets*: all which appeares in another place of this
booke, and the juft caufes of their proceedings annexed thereunto.
Laftly in this *pag.* hee tels us of his hardfhip divers nights together,
that himfelfe and the reft of his mutinous companions, as *Weekes,
Holden, &c.* endured, which was juft with God and man, for extream
evils muft have extreame remedies, and yet tis well knowne tis not
a full dayes journey from *Roade Ifland* to *Providence.* And whereas
a ftranger would thinke hee was then forced to goe to *Nanhiganfet-
Bay* amongft the Indians, hee went not from *Providence* till they
were as weary of thefe Mutineeres as either *Plimouth* or *Roade Ifland*
had beene before them.

And becaufe hee often mentioneth the hard meafure hee received
at *Plimouth,* ftill carrying it on as if difference in Religion had beene
the ground of it: I thought good here to give the Reader to underftand what was the ground of his troubles there, that fo all men may
know what Religion this man is of: for the tree is beft knowne by
its fruite. The firft complaint that came againft him for which hee
was brought before authority, was by Mr. *Ralph Smith* a Minifter,
who

who being of *Gortons* acquaintance received him with his family into his houſe, with much humanity and Chriſtian reſpect,promiſing
him as free uſe of it as himſelfe, &c. but Mr. *Gorton*-becomming
troubleſome, (after meanes uſed to remove the offences taken
by Mr. *Smith,* but to no purpoſe, growing ſtill more inſolent) Mr.
Smith deſired him to provide elſewhere for himſelfe *:* but *Gorton*
refuſed, ſaying, hee had as good intereſt in the houſe as Mr. *Smith*
had. And when hee was brought before Authority, ſtood ſtoutly
to maintaine it to our amaſement. But was ordered to depart and
provide other wayes by a time appointed. And not long after
there comming a woman of his acquaintance to *Plimouth,* divers
came to the Governour with complaints againſt her, being a ſtran-
ger,for unworthy and offenſive ſpeeches and carriages uſed by her.
Whereupon theGovernour ſent to her to know herbuſineſſe,&c.and
commanded her departure, and ordered the Sea-man that brought
her, to returne her to the place from whence ſhee came,at his next
paſſage thither. But *Gorton* ſaid ſhee ſhould not goe, for hee had
occaſion to employ her, &c. Hereupon the Governour (it being in
the time of a Court) ſent for him, and becauſe hee had hidde her,
ſtood in juſtification of his practiſeand refuſed to obey the command
of the Court (who ſeconded the Governours order.) He was committed till hee could procure ſureties for his good behaviour till the
next Court which was a generall Court, and there to anſwer to this
contempt. The time being come and the Court ſet, *Gorton* was
called; But the Governour being wearied with ſpeech to other
cauſes,requeſted one of his Aſſiſtants who was preſent at his commitment and privy to the whole cauſe to declare the ſame. This
Aſſiſtant no ſooner ſtood up to ſhew the Country the cauſe of his
bonds in the great affront hee had given the Government, but *Gorton* ſtretching out his hand towards his face ſaid with a loud voice,
*If Satan will accuſe the brethren, let him come downe from Jehoſhuabs
right hand and ſtand here,* And that done,in a ſeditious manner turned himſelfe to the people and ſaid, with his armes ſpread abroad;
*Yee ſee good people how yee are abuſed! Stand for your liberty; And let
them not bee parties and judges ,*with many otheropprobriousſpeeches
ofthatkinde. Hereupondivers Elders of Churches being preſent,de-
ſiring leave of the Governour to ſpeake, complaining of his ſeditious carriage,and requeſted theCourt not to ſuffer theſe abuſes,butto
inflict condigne puniſhment. And yet notwithſtanding all wee did

[Errata: l. 37, for complain- ing, read, com- plained.]

to

to him was but to take the forfeiture of his forefaid bonds for his good behaviour.   Nay being but low and poore in his eftate, wee tooke not above eight or ten pounds of it, left it might lie too heavy upon his wife and children.   But he muft either get new fureties for the behaviour till the next generall Court, or fuch time as he departed the Government, or lie in prifon till hee could : now hee knowing his outragious paffions which hee could not reftraine, procured fureties, but immediately left *Plimouth* and went to *Roade Ifland*, where upon complaint of our perfecutions hee found prefent reliefe there: yet foone afterward he abufed them in a greater meafure and had heavier yet too light a punifhment inflicted on him, and all for breach of the civill peace and notorious contempt of Authority without the leaft mention of any points of Religion on the Governments part, but as before.

And whereas in *pag.* 4. Mr. *Gorton* further accufeth us that they were deprived and taken away from their quiet poffeffions, &c. Such was his carriage at *Plimouth* and *Providence* at his firft fettling as neither of the Governments durft admit or receive him into cohabitation, but refufed him as a peft to all focieties. Againe in the fame *pag.* he accufeth *Maffachufets* and *Plimouth* to have denyed them to be in our Government, *but when wee perceived the place to bee a refuge for fuch as were oppreffed then, &c.* 'Tis true that *Plimouth* gave way to Mr. *Williams* and his company to fit downe at *Providence* and have never molefted them to this day, but refufed *Gorton* and *Weekes*, &c. upon *Weekes* his follicitation when I was at *Providence* for the reafons before mentioned, &c. And for thofe particular relations he makes of *Robert Cole, William Arnold*, and *Benedict* his fonne, I wave, as not being fo well acquainted with their cafes, but fee hee writes with a venomous pen; onely take notice he would make it a great crime in them to trade on the Sabbath (as it is) when himfelfe at that time denyed the fanctification of it.

In *pag.* 5. hee complaines that powder was traded to the Indians and denyed to them.   *Anfw.* If it were traded to the Indians, for my part I approve it not, it being againft the expreffe law of the Country, and a large penalty annexed: but there was good reafon to refufe it to them which held fuch familiarity with Malignant Indians efpecially during the time of their confederacy againft us.

In *pag.* 6. he fpeakes as if hee had beene under fome cenfure of the
Maffachufets

Maffachufets at the time of the warrant there by him fpecified, how truly copied I know not: but am fure at this time he was perfonally under no cenfure of theirs.

In *pag.* 7. hee accufeth Magiftrates and Minifters for bringing in all the accufations that came in againft them.Who but publique perfons fhould take notice of publique infolencies? And as for Mr. *Collens* his ftory I am a ftranger to, but beleeve it is mifreported as well as others.

In *pag.* 8. hee manifefts hee durft not live under a forraigne Prince, meaning the Dutch, having never been falfe to his King and Country, &c. with many ignorant fwelling words; as if it were treafon to ones Prince to live under a forraigne State though an Ally.   And in the fame *pag.* hee would lay the death of Miftris *Hutchenfon* who was mother in law to Mr. *Collens,*on us: although they went from *Road Ifland* which is not under the *Maffachufets* where fhee had lived fome yeares after her remove from the *Bay,* and not from the *Maffachufets* to the Dutch of her owne accord where they were cut offby the Indians.

In *pag.* 9. he fhewes how they bought lands of *Myantonimo* Prince of thofe parts.   *Anfw.* 1. Hee was not the Prince of that part as was proved publiquely at *Maffachufets* himfelfe being prefent. 2. He had no proper right in it, as is fhewed at large elfewhere.

In the fame *pag.* he beginneth a large letter full of railing blafphemies which continueth to *pag.*31. and however it bee not exactly fet downe as it was fent,yet I admire at Gods providence, for hee is falne into the fnare he laid,this being brought againft him to accufe him of blafphemy, before a Committee of Parliament, who called in his book,and referred him to the Houfe,&c.but I forbeare to fhew his folly here, which is referred to another place and his wickedneffe difcovered therein.

In *pag.* 32. hee faith the Government of the *Maffachufets* had no fhew of any thing againft them but Religion, and yet the whole carried on in his owne way as well as what wee now print, fhewes it was in the right of two Indian *Sachims,* namely *Pumham* and *Socononoco,* who placing themfelves under the protection cfthe *Maffachufets* complained of violence offered them by Mr. *Gorton*and his company, it being our manner both in Capitals and Criminals to doe them the like juftice wee doe one to another, wherein walking by the fame rules of righteoufneffe towards them, they
have

have the leffe caufe to take offence at us.

From *pag*.33. forward, are many Letters which I cannot beleeve al is in them, and therfore remain jealous of his fincerity in Printing them.

In *pag*.37. hee holds forth converfion to be the ground of the *Maffachufets* fending to them, now to that end, faith hee, they fent a Minifter. 'Tis true, there was a gracious young man one Mr. *Joh. Bulkley* then a Student, but in no miniftery, went to teach to the Company they fent to guard their owne Commiffioners, and to bring in *Gorton* if need required: but I dare not beleeve what hee affirmes. And for the Copy of a Letter hee fathers upon the Commiffioners fent by the Government of the *Maffachufet*; I conclude 'tis rather fet downe upon memory then right, becaufe of fome atteftations I have by me to make ufe on elfewhere, which feeme to hold forth the contrary, and fo I doe not credit it.

In *pag*. 38, & 39. hee relates how their wives were frighted at mens prefenting their muskets at them, &c. and fuffering fuch hardfhips as occafioned death, &c. Which muft alfo bee falfe, for honeft men have depofed there was no fuch prefentment, and that their wives came freely and familiarly to them, both before and after they were taken. So alfo hee affirmes our men would allow of no parley but private, or elfe they would difpatch them in a quarter of an houre, which I will never beleeve, becaufe I know the men to bee men fearing God, and durft not proceed as hee relateth it.

In *pag*. 40, & 41. he alfo taxeth the Commiffioners and fouldiers with breach of Covenants in time of treaty, as, *breaking open their houfes, desks, killing their cattle, &c.* All which is falfe, for oath is made to the contrary, which I fhall make ufe of before my Lord of *Warwick* Governour in chiefe, and the reft of the honourable Committee for foraign Plantations in due time and place, that whereas they were by agreement to have two houfes for their company being about 40 men, they made ufe of but one, nor did any of thefe things laid to their charge.

In *pag*.45. he would make *Pumham* and *Socononoco*, the naturall fubjects of *Myantonimo* their Prince; but this was difproved. And in the fame page, he faith, the Magiftrates fuggefted to the people' as though there were *feare of fome combination between the Indians and them. Anfw.* I dare not fay you had a hand in the depth of their confpiracy: but this I thinke you dare not deny, that *Weekes* one

of

of your ftouteft Champions, lent *Myantonimo* an Armour,in which he was taken in battell againft *Uncus*, who was under the protecti-on of the Englifh united Colonies: for which *Uncus* put him to death;and in your own book you hold forth more familiarity then becomes you.

But here it will bee neceffary for mee to fhew you the ground of this warre.   There was a people called by the name of the *Pecoats*, being a ftout warlike people, who had been at warre with the *Na-nohigganfets* many yeares, and were too ftrong for them; fo alfo were they at fome diftance of affection with this *Uncus*, who was *Sachim* of a people called the *Mohegans*, neare the head of a River falleth into the fea at *Pecoat*.   The chiefe *Sachim* of this people of *Pecoat*, was called *Tatobam*, a ftout man.   The *Nanohigganfets* and thefe ftrove who fhould be greateft.   This *Tatobam* envied the En-glifh, and was the firft ftirrer and contriver of this generall Plot, that they might all joyne together to deftroy the Englifh; but the *Nanohigganfets* refufed to joyne with them, knowing if that were once done, the next ruine muft be their owne.   Afterward having fubdued many fmall peoples, and one as great as themfelves, and and fome Englifh planting more neare then the body of our Planta-tions, though without wrong to him, or any of them, hee cut off Captaine *Stone* his Barke and Company, and after this killed divers ftragling Englifh.   This ftirred up the Englifh to take revenge: The *Nanohigganfets* and *Uncus*, *Sachim* of the *Moheges* feeing this,becaufe it was againft their comon Enemy,offered their fervice to joyn with the Englifh: the *Nanohigganfets* did no confiderable fervice in com-parifon of the *Moheges*, who did as much as could bee expected,but the *Nanohigganfets* rather gathered up the fpoile, to the great offence of the *Englifh* and *Moheges*, feldome ingaging in any fight.   The Englifh killed and deftroyed this people utterly, fo that thofe that were left remaining utterly deferted the Countrey, and the Englifh wonne it, and are now poffeffed of it.   After this victory, *Myan-tonimo Sachim* or Lord of the *Nanohigganfets*,and *Uncus* Lord of the *Moheges*, manifefted no good blood towards each other; the En-glifh at *Hartford* where the Government for *Coneetacut* is held, hea-ring of it, got them together, and made a peace and threefold Co-venant between the Government of *Coneetacut*, *Nanohigganfet*, and *Mohege*, which was figned by the Governour of *Coneetacut*, *Myan-tonimo Sachim* of *Nanohigganfet*, and *Uncus Sachim* of *Mohegan*. The
Cove-

Covenants ran to this purpofe, To confirme their League between the Englifh and them, and either to other, and to hold forth a league of perpetuall peace between them. And in cafe any difference fhould arife between thefe two Indian *Sachims*, or their people, the party offended fhould complaine to the Governour of *Coneetacut*,who was to mediate and to determine the controverfie between his two friends and their people: And in cafe the injury were great, and the party wronging would not ftand to the forefaid award and determination, then it fhould not onely bee lawfull for the wronged to right himfelfe by force of Armes, but for the Englifh party alfo to affift the innocent in that kind. And to this they all firmed as before.

The *Nanohigganfet Sachim* never regarded this Covenant, the *Mohege Sachim* ever faithfully obferved it. But *Myantonimo* of *Nanohigganfet* had thoughts now to profecute the *Pecoats* defigne, and to deftroy the Englifh, (the *Pecoets* Nation being rooted out by Gods juft judgement as before) and travels farre and neare to draw all the Indians in the Countrey into this horrid confederacy with him; but this *Uncus* would not bee wonne, though he would have taken his daughter in marriage, but ever acquainted the Englifh with his working. At length an inferiour *Sachim*, fubordinate to *Nanohigganfet* affronts him and his men,hee complaines to the Englifh, they fend to this inferiour *Sachim*, hee fleights their admonition,goes on his courfe ; whereupon the other demands leave to make warre upon him, not requiring any aide. Still the Englifh forewarne the other party of the evill they were like to bring upon themfelves;till at length they profeffe theyhave had peace enough,& now it is time to war. Whereupon the Englifh give way to *Vncus* to revenge himfelfe, he doth it; the other are beaten. Now *Myantonimo* he prepares an Army of above 1000 men, and comes upon a fudden upon *Uncus* without any refpect to Covenants, and took *Uncus* at advantage, not with above 300 men; by which meanes they befet him every way in his Fort, which ftands upon a point of Land between two Rivers. *Myantonimo* fo difperfed his men to prevent their flight, as *Uncus* making a defperate falley with almoft his full force, routed the other, flew neare upon an hundred, and forced them tofly: But Mr. *Weekes* one of *Samuel Gortons* company (as I am credibly informed) lending the Great*Sachim* a complete Armor; and having it on in the fight, was not able to fly fo faft as his men,

and

and was taken by this meanes. Yet fuch was *Uncus* refpect ftill to
the Englifh, as hee kept him till hee fent to the Englifh, *viz.* to the
Right Worfhipfull *George Fenwicke* Efquire, to know what he fhould
doe with him, who lived next to him, Hee wifhed him to follow
their owne Cuftome, and to deale with him, as if hee had not advifed with him, or there were no Englifh in the land to advife withall. Hereupon hee refolved to have killed him forthwith, according to their Cuftome. But no fooner were the *Nanohigganfets* got
home, who had loft divers Sachims, Captaines, and chiefe men in
this fight, but they fend to Mr. *Gorton*, &c. who fent a Note to *Uncus*, with a command by the bearer, that they put him not to death,
but ufe him kindly and returne him. This the Meffenger either faid
or they fuppofed came from the *Maffachufets* Governour, and did
much daunt *Uncus* and his men: but to cleare up all, they advifed
with the Gent. of *Coneetacut*, who wifhed him to keep him prifoner, and to advife with the Commiffioners of the United Colonies
whereof they were part, whofe meeting would bee ere long by
courfe at the *Maffachufets*:which counfell hee followed, and entrea-
ted the Governour of *Coneetacut* (*Myantonimo* alfo defiring it) to
keep him fafe for him till then, whereupon hee was brought to
Hartford: And many gifts were fent to the prifoner; which hee
beftowed like himfelfe, fome on him that took him, fome on *Uncus*,
fome on his wife, fome on *Uncus* brother being a great Captaine,
and fome on others where he had received kindneffes, and this was
all the ranfome was paid, there being not fo much as a ranfome
propofed by the *Nanohigganfets*, nor fet down by *Uncus*. But hee
advifing with the Commiffioners, theyconfidering how many ways
befides open hoftility he had fought the life of *Uncus*, by poyfon,
fecret murther, witchcraft, &c. advifed him to put him to death,
there being no fafety for him whilft hee lived, being fo reftleffe in
his practice againft his life; and therefore wifhed *Uncus* to proceed
with him according to their owne Cuftome towards prifoners of
Warre, which is to put them to death; according to which advice
he proceeded,knowing now that none of the *Engl.* would intercede
for him. And hereupon *Uncus* went to *Hartford* and demanded
his prifoner, and led him to an houfe of his owne, out of the limits of the Englifh, and there killed him, where was an Englifh
man or two by to prevent their accuftomed cruelties, in cutting off
not onely the head and hands of their prifoners when they are
dead,

dead, and make bracelets of the fore-joints of their fingers,&c. but to torture them whilft living with moft inhumane cruelties. After this, the *Nanohigganfets* would warre upon him in revenge of his death; wee forbade them,and at our next meeting of Commiffioners to confult about the Weale publike of the United Colonies, in regard the*Nanohigganfets* pleaded they had taken a ranfome for his life, and his life alfo, which the other denyed; Wee fent for *Uncus*, and fent to the great *Sachims* of *Nanohigganfet* to come alfo, or appeare by Commiffioners;but they fent foure Commiffioners with full authority to treate, where we found neither ranfome, nor colour of ranfome in the leaft meafure.And fo a truce was agreed on, & if *Uncus* brake it,we were then freed from our engagement to defend him any further, for they defired no more: And if the *Nanohigganfets* broke it, then it fhould be lawfull for us the United Colonies to take part with him, &c. But the truth is, though before they had fo neare neighbours of the Englifh, as *Gorton*, &c. and till *Myantonimo's* Government, as they were the moft in number, and moft peaceable of all the *Indians*, yet now they werechanged, as if they had not been the people, and had their Tutors, Secretaries, and promptors to fuggeft their greatneffe and our weakneffe to them, as his Book witneffeth, in fuch manner as I am confident if the *Gortonians* (for I take the phrafe from his owne Book here, never hearing it before) bee fuffered to live fo neare them, it will bee our ruine, or thefe *Indians*(which we defire not)in fhort time. I thought good to infert this Narration thus briefly, that the Reader might underftand the ground of his many charges, calling God to witneffe I know not the leaft falfhood related in it, but many things for brevities fake omitted worthy a hiftory;but I am now about an anfwer, not an hiftory,and therefore thus briefe. But to return.

In *pag.* 47. fee how he fcoffes at the Sabbath as if there were no other ground for our religious obfervation of it, then Mr. *Cottons* judgement. And in *pag.* 48. hee is full of many fcoffs, as if hee and his *Gortonians* would not, nor did fhoot at all, when as I have oath to prove they fhot alfo at the other, but the truth is, I heard fome fay that their powder was fo dampe and moift as they could not without great difficulty difcharge a peece, which I well beleeve might bee the reafon they fhot no more then they did.

In *pag.* 49. hee chargeth Captaine *Cooke* with breach of Articles: And yet I have it attefted upon oath,that there were none agreed on;
onely

onely they defired they might not goe bound; which was eafily
affented to, they behaving themfelves quietly. And for their cattle, I never heard the number to be fo great by farre; but asking the
Governour of the *Maffachufets* about them, hee profeffed they did
not amount to halfe their charges. And if any aske by what authority they went out of their own Government to do fuch an act?
Know that his former feditious and turbulent carriage in all parts
where he came, as *Plymouth, Roade-Ifland*, a place of greateft liberty,
Providence that place which relieved him in that his fo great extremity, and his fo defperate clofe with fo dangerous and potent enemies, and at fuch a time of Confpiracy by the fame Indians, together with the wrongs done to the Indians, and English under the
protection of that Government of the *Maffachufets*, who complained and defired reliefe; together with his notorious contempt
of all Civill Government, as well as that particular, and his blafphemies againft God needlefly manifefted in his proud letters to
them, one whereof hee hath printed, and the other I have herewith
publifhed for him. All thefe confidered, you fhall fee hereby caufe
enough, why they proceeded againft him as a common enemy of
the Countrey. And as fuch an one, the faid Commiffioners being
then met together at *Maffachufets* by courfe, for the Weale of the
whole, upon juft complaint ordered and thought meet that the
Government of the *Maffachufets* fhould call them to accompt, and
proceed with them fo farre as ftood with righteoufneffe and juftice:
And by their declaration thou maift eafily fee they went no further,
for they refufing fafe conduct to come to anfwer to the matters a-
gainft them, forced them upon this charge needlefly, which they
made them beare part of as before. So that here's caufe enough befides blafphemy for their proceeding with them I fuppofe.

In *pag.* 51. he chargeth *New-Engl.* Minifters to pray in the ftreets:
but take notice I have been there thefe 26 yeares, and better, but
never heard of fuch a practife, till I now reade it in his Book.

In *pag.* 52. he faith, the Governour to fatisfie the people, faid, *we
were apprehended for divers groffe opinions*, &c. *Anfw.* You may
fee in the laft Section but one there was caufe enough. And yet for
Opinions, let mee tell you that you held, That that Image of God
after which man was created was Chrift; and that when *Adam* fell
Chrift was flaine, &c. And as for your opinion concerning Churches, Mr. *Williams* by way of fad complaint told me, you denyed
any

any true Churches of Chrift to bee in the world: alfo Baptifme it
felfe, and the Lords Supper, Sabbath, Magiftracy as it was an ordinance ufed amongft Chriftians.   And for the Lords Supper, that
it is but a fpell, the Minifters Necromancers, and the Commu-
nicants drunke with the juice of the grape, &c.   And for this laft
paffage here mentioned, the Reader fhall have it at large in a fecond
Letter fent by him and his companions to the Government of the
Maffachufets, concealed by himfelf in his Book, though he pretend-
eth to have printed all, &c.

In *pag.* 53. as he abufeth others, fo Mr. *Cotton* and Mr. *Ward,* in
affirming that Mr. *Ward* put himfelfe into a paffion, and ftirred up
Carder to recant, &c. as being no difcredit to him, becaufe Mr. *Cotton* ordinarily preached that publiquely once a yeare, whichthe next
yeare he recants, &c.   But Mr. *Ward* being in Towne, a man well
knowne and reputed, I fhewed him the Booke, and hee gave mee
thanks, and returned this anfwer to it *verbatim* : Samuel Gorton
having made mee a Margent note in the 53 page *of his Booke, I hold my
felf called to make this anfwer to it; I cannot call to minde that ever I
knew or fpake with fuch a man as* Richard Carder, *nor that ever I had
any fpeech with any prifoner at a window, nor fhould I need it in* New-
England, *where there is liberty enough given for conference with prifoners
in more free and convenient places.   This I remember, that one* Robert
Potter *who went in the fame Ship with mee into* New-England, *and ex-
preffing by the way fo much honefty and godlineffe as gained my good
opinion and affection towards him: I hearing that hee was affected with*
Samuel Gortons *blafphemous conceits and carriages, and therefore now
imprifoned with him, I went to vifit him, and having free fpeech with
him in the open prifon yard, who fhedding many teares might happily move
me to expreffe my affection to him, which* Samuel Gorton *calls paffion:
After fome debate about his new opinions, I remember I ufed a fpeech to
him to this effect: That hee fhould doe well and wifely to make fuch acknowledgement of his errours as his confcience would permit; telling him
that Mr.* Cotton *whom hee had fo much reverenced in* Old England,
and New, *had given him a godly example in that kinde, by a publique
acknowledgement upon a folemne Faft day with many teares; That in the
time when errours were fo ftirring, God leaving him for a time, he fell into a
fpirituall flumber; and had it not been for the watchfulneffe of his brethren the Elders, &c. hee might have flept on; and bleffed God very cor-
dially for awakening him, and was very thankefull to his Brethren, for*
                                                                    their

their watchfulnesse over him, and faithfulnesse towards him:wherein hee honoured God not a little, and greatly rejoyced the hearts of his hearers; and therefore it would bee no shame for him to doe the like.

Concerning Mr. Cotton, *were I worthy, I would presume to speake that now of him, which I have said more then many times of him elswhere, That I hold him such an eminent Worthy of Christ, as very few others have attained unto him; and that I hold my selfe not worthy to wipe his slippers for matters of grace, learning, and industry in the worke of God.*

For the Author Samuel Gorton, *my self and others farre more judicious, take him to bee a man whose spirit is starke drunke with blasphemies and insolencies, a corrupter of the Truth, and a disturber of the Peace where ever hee comes; I intreat him to read* Titus 1. 13. *with an humble heart, and that is the greatest harm I wish him.*

N. W.

Thus much of the Answer and testimony of that Reverend and Grave Divine, wherein the Reader may see how Mr. *Gorton* abuseth all men, by casting mire and dirt in the faces of our best deserving Instruments.

In *page.* 54. he accuseth Mr. *Wilson* and Mr. *Cotton* for stirring up the people against them, &c. *Answ.* What they pressed in their Sermons, I was not present to heare; but this I can affirme, that from the time of their liberty to my departure from *New England*, which is not much above two moneths, I have heard many precious godly men affirme, that *Sam.* Gorton and his company needlesly in their writings and conference belched out such blasphemy as they thought God was offended with the Country for giving them the liberty they had. And that you may the better see his carriage, (it being the manner of the Countrey to let their prisoners come to heare the Word preached) Mr. *Gorton*, &c. being there after Mr. *Cotton* had ended his Sermon on a Sabbath day, asked leave to speake, which Mr. *Cotton* assenting to, the Governour being present gave him leave, where with a loud voice before the whole Congregation being very great, hee declared, *That the Ministery of the Word, Sacraments, Censures, and other Ordinances of Religion in the hands of Ministers, are like the silver Shrines of* Diana *in the hands of the craftsmen of Ephesus,&c.* And if the truth of this be questioned, I have testimony upon Oath to make it good.

In *pag.* 55, 56, 57. many things might bee excepted against, as

first

in *p.* 55.his great refpect manifefted to that government,becaufe derived from the State of *England,*which what it was thou maift largely
fee in certaine Obfervations of a godly Divine annexed hereunto,
upon his owne two contemptuous and blafphemous Letters, or
rather Bookes, wherein are 48 feverall afperfions caft on them.
Secondly,hisappealing,*pag.*56.from their Juftice when their Charter enjoynes none.

In *pag.* 56,&57,the Queftions as hee hath fet them downe, and
the relation about the time allowed him to give his anfwer; I queftion whether he have dealt fairely therein, becaufe hee is fo often
found faulty.

To paffe by his Anfwer, and his large explanation of himfelfe,
*pag.*58.and come to 59. &c. and fo the reft of his Anfwers to the
Queftions to 64. I anfwer, though I know not whether hee doe
right as hee ftates things; yet this I know, being attefted by reverend perfons, That hee then maintained, *that God made man after*
his owne image; and that God hath but one image, and that is Chrift; and
this was the Incarnation of Chrift, his exinanition by which we are faved.
And when it was objected, wee are not faved by the incarnation of
Chrift, but by the death of Chrift. *True, faith hee, therefore* Adam
fell, and fo deftroyed Gods image,and that was the death of Chrift. When
it was objected againe, *Adams* fall was not our falvation, but con-
demnation, but the death of Chrift was our falvation: and therefore *Adams* fall could not be the death of Chrift. Hee would by
no meanes either revoke or explaine his fpeech (though much ur-
ged thereunto) to agree with the principles of Chriftian Religion.
Being further demanded what he then thought of that Chrift in
whom we beleeve,borne of the *Virgin Mary,*and who fuffered under
Pontius Pilate? He anfwered,*That that Chrift was a fhadow, and but*
arefemblance of what is done in mee and every true Chriftian. And now
judge good Reader, whether this be like what hee mentioneth , or
whether it were a trifle not worthy the mentioning: But if he will
be fo unfaithfull as to omit it, I dare not.

As for his cenfure, *pag.* 64, I know not whether it bee right
fet downe ; and fo the charge,*pag.*65.wherein I dare fay he wron-
geth the Minifters, in faying; *They ftirred up the people to famifh*
them.

As for his long and tedious Letter to Mr. *Green,* from *page 66* to
74. I paffe it by, as he faith Mr. *Green* did. But in 74. hee would
make

make it an afperfion upon Mr. *Endecot* for faying *that God had ftirred them up to goe out of their owne jurifdiction to fetch them from their owne places.* Take notice as it is litterally within the line of *Plimouth* Government in their Grant, yet the Indians before mentioned having fubjected themfelves to the *Maffachufets*, the Commiffioners for *Plimouth* as well as thofe for *Coneetacut*, and *New-Haven*, upon the manifold complaints and reafons before mentioned, being met together at their ordinary time and place appointed and ordered it fhould bee fo, as appeares by the copy of their act.

At a meeting of the Commiffioners for the United Colonies of *New-England* holden at *Bofton* the feventh of *September* 1643.

Whereas complaints have beene made againft Samuel Gorton *and his company, and fome of them weighty and of great confequence; And whereas the faid* Gorton *and the reft have beene formerly fent for, and now lately by the generall Court of the* Maffachufets *with a fafe conduct both for their comming and returne, that they might give anfwer and fatisfaction wherein they have done wrong. If yet they fhall ftubbornely refufe, the Commiffioners for the United Colonies think fit that the Magiftrates in the* Maffachu-fets *proceed againft them according to what they fhall finde juft ; and the reft of the Jurisdictions will approve and concurre in what fhall bee fo warrantably done, as if their Commiffioners had beene prefent at the conclufions, provided that this conclufion doe not prejudice the Government of* Plimouth *in any right they can juftly claime unto any Tract or Tracts, &c.*

By which Order it appeares they were ftirred up and allowed by *Plimouth* it felfe as well as the reft, as afore, to fend for and deale with as indeed the common difturbers of the peace of the Country.

[Errata: l. 26, for with as indeed, read with them as indeed.]

And whereas in *pag.* 76. He complaineth of the Governours laft order for breaking the order of Court, yet take it as he relates it and any underftanding man will eafily fee on the other fide the fame leafe that they ftill were bound to the reft of the Articles at their confinement, which they were now in a high way to break. And for that little Ifland called *Roade Ifland* they were forced to fhelter in, take notice 'tis 30 miles about, very fruitfull, and plentifully abounding with all manner of food the Country affordeth, and hath

hath two Townes beſides many great Farmes well ſtocked in the ſame.

In *pag.*79. Hee complaines of us for calling them *Gortonians,* and ſo theIndians calling them*Gortonoges* and notEngliſhmen,with many affected foppiſh vanities, phraſes and termes I never heard on before, and yet have lived in *New-England* from the beginning, being now above 26 yeares. I wiſh hee ſtudy not, nor affect theſe things, but I much feare it.

In *pag.* 80.   Hee tels a tale of a tub , of *Myantonimo's* being ſlain as hee marched, which is falſe, for hee was put to death, and in an houſe, but not upon a march. And is it to bee wondered at, that two Engliſh were preſent to ſee the manner of their proceeding in ſo weighty a cauſe as one Prince putting another his perfidious enemy and captive to death, eſpecially when they were required by the Commiſſioners to forbeare their accuſtomed torments and to give him honourable buriall, which they did and had thanks returned by the *Nanhigganſets* for thoſe particulars. Now if any would know how it was done? It was onely at one blow with an hatchet on the ſide of the heade as hee walked eaſily in the roome (expecting no leſſe) which fully diſpatched him at once. And thus mnch for anſwer to this charge.

To let paſſe *pag.* 81. what hee ſaith about *Myantonimo's* death as being anſwered before, and come to *pag.* 82.&c. where he mentioneth a conſultation held amongſt the Indians to put themſelves under the ſubjection of the State of *England,* &c.   *Anſw.* Wee heard indeed of this deſperate plot by this unfaithfull people, who had beene in Covenant with the ſeverall Governments long before, but never obſerved any one Article farther then it might further their owne deſigne which was to bee abſolute Lords of the Country though with the ruine of us all.And truly had he not publiſhed this and the following diſcourſe wee could never have proved it though wee heard of it both from Engliſh and Indians. And however *My-antonimo* dyed, yet the plot liveth and continueth to this day. Now though I dare not ſay, nor doe I thinke they joyne with them in aiming at the ruine of all the Engliſh, yet they joyne with them in many of their Councels, contrive their ſturdy anſwers by writings, and become their Secretaries. Who knowes not that they cannot write? and who knowes not their owne anſwers from thoſe that come under your hands? And if the State of *England* (which
God

God defend) fhould eftablifh your and their joynt propofitions: then were their plot accomplifhed: for they might and would worke freely our ruine when as wee might not take up armes againft them, but by vertue of warrant or writ from hence procured upon our complaints here, which alfo would bee fix months in ordinary courfe in procuring and returning, when as in one of thefe all our throates might bee cut, and thofe hopefull beginnings fo much favoured by our gracious God hitherto in a high way to bee overthrowne. Indeed wee heard further , and for my part I beleeve it, that for the better accomplifhment hereof, *Samuel Gorton* and fome of his company had perfwaded the *Nanohigganfets* to fend the King a very large Prefent of Beaver and otter skins which they fhould bring in, and accordingly did: but withall the Englifh reporter faith, that if he could finde favour with the Parliament, then hee would reft there: but if they frowned on him, hee doubted not to but obtaine what was meet from the King. But the times would not fuffer him to publifh this alfo, elfe I fee wee fhould have had all: and this take notice of, That (as the fame report teftified) at his departure hee wifhed them by no meanes to warre with us the *United Colonies*,but compound though it coft them never fo deare, but affured them at his returne hee would come ftrengthened with fuch authority and fo many of his friends as that the *Nanohigganfets* and themfelves fhould not need to feare any thing the reft of the Englifh could doe. And that we heard thefe things from credible teftimony and are not faigned by mee, I take the fearcher of the heart to witneffe, yea fay further that I beleeve them to bee true.

His glorious feeming well-deferving acts follow in *pag.* 82. &c. to 89. but note that *Weekes, Holden,* and *Warner,* (though I leaft know the laft, but am fure for the other two) were his ftrong Affiftants in his former feditious and mutinous carriages both at *Roade Ifland* and *Providence,* and therefore fit Commiffioners as he terms them, for the accomplifhing fuch a defigne. And in *pag.*85.note firft, their complyance with the *Nanohigganfets,* and his falfe relation in faying *Myantonimo's* ranfome was taken and his life alfo, which is moft falfe, as I made appeare in my former relation. And for the Kings being our and their Judge,as in *pag.* 86. Know the Indians care no more for the King then they doe for us, whom they would deftroy if they could.

And in *pag.* 88. take notice of the *Gortonifts* complying and joyning

ing with them, firft, by calling them their *fellow-fubjeɛts*, and fecondly, fpeaking of the *Maukquagges* (whom wee ordinarily call
Mo-whakes) as being the *moſt fierce and warlike people in the Country,
where (faith hee) wee are furniſhed with* 3700 *Guns, men expert in the
ufe of them, &c.*   Now thefe indeed as the Switzers ferve for hire.
And the *Nanohigganfets* being rich have hired them to affift them in
their warre.   But though the *Gortonifts* it feemes are interefted with
the *Nanohigganfets* in their ftrength againft us, yet are they neither fo
many men nor have fo many arms, but have too many and are very
expert in them; being continually fupplyed by the French and
Dutch, whofe aime is chiefly at the trade of Furs, and hereby not
onely robbe us of that fhould helpe to maintaine our plantations
which are growing up into a Nation, but furnifh the Indians with
all manner of armes, which I would to God, and humbly befeech
this High Court of Parliament to take into ferious confideration,
and treate with their feverall Ambaffadors about it, as a thing un-
reafonable in it felfe, and fuch as hath beene pernicious to French
and Dutch, and may bee deftruɛtive to them and us, if fome due
courfe bee not taken.   But to returne from my humble requeft to
the State, to my anfwer to *Samuel Gorton*; although this be a moft unworthy vaunt of his, yet I truft the State will make fuch ufe of it as
never to fuffer this defperate crew to live fo neere our malicious enemies the *Nanohiganf.* and that they will not only countenance the fentence of the *Maffachuf.* Government againft them, but hinder the faid
Gortons returne thither, by forbidding him to fet foot on that land
of *New-England* he hath filled with fo many troubles in all the parts
where he hath beene.
    In *pag.* 91. Hee taxeth *Plimouth* to joyne with the *Maffachufets* to
fruftrate their Government by vertue of their new Charter.   'Tis
true, we would have had the *Maffachufets* to have then fent, and rendered a reafon to the State of their proceedings, knowing as before
that Mr. *Gortons* journey was for evill and not for good: but they
being then taken up with more weighty concernments negleɛted it:
but *Plimouth* did then petition the right honourable *Robert* Earle of
Warwicke the Governour in chiefe of the Englifh plantations in *A-
merica* and the reft of that honourable Committee joyned in Commiffion with him, that wee might enjoy our ancient limits of Government granted in our letters Patent, and withall fhewed that
their Charter for the limits of it now granted, was contained
                                                                within

within our line of Government: and truft I fhall now receive an-fwer. Tis true alfo that we fent Mr. *John Brown* furnifhed with thefe following inftruction to fignifie to all that were intereffed in that new erected Government as followeth by Commiffion given at *New-Plimouth, Nov.* 8. 1644.

1. That a great part of their fuppofed Government is within the line of the Government of New-Plimouth.

2. That wee affuredly knew that this ever to bee honoured Houfe of Parliament would not, nor will when they fhall know of it, take from us the moft ancient Plantation, any part of the line of our Government formerly granted; it being contrary to their Principles.

3. To forbid them and all and every of them to exercife any authority or power of Government within the limits of our Letters Patents.

4. To certifie them that Coweefet *is not onely within the faid limits, but that the* Sachim *thereof and his fonnes have taken protection of this our Government. And therefore to forbid them to enter upon any part of his or their lands without due order and leave from our Government.*

Now thefe inftructions were figned by the Governour. And Mr. *Browne* going to *Roade Ifland* for this end came very feafonable when a publique meeting was appointed for your new Magiftrates and people,(but as he reported,for a moft vile end; *viz.*to take into confideration a new difpofall of the lands formerly given out, as if fome had too much andfome too little,& for now refpect of perfons, and their eftates was to bee laid afide.) And here note that Mr. *Cod-dington,* Mr. *Briuton, &c.* that we at *Plimouth* had fpeciall eye to, when wee commended them thither,abhorred their courfe, abftain-ed from their meetings,looked upon themfelves as perfons in great danger, and bemoaned their condition to divers their friends, being now overwhelmed with cares and feares what would bee the iffue of things. And note that now alfo Mr. *Samuel Gorton* that before had fuffered fo much by authority for his evill doing, and was come to deny it and preach againft it , being now by thefe Inhabi-tants called to place, accepts it, and became a Magiftrate amongft them, &c. But whereas hee intimates, as if Mr. *Browne* had onely done his meffage (according to his inftructions) in a private way from houfe to houfe, therein hee wrongs him: for hee did it pub-liquely in the place of their Affembly, who were fo daunted at it as they brake up, and did no act intended for that day , as hee rela-ted it: but fome would have had him imprifoned,others punifhed,

[Errata: l. 24, for & put (.]

others

others fent to the Dutch and fo for England.   Yea Mr. *Gorton* himfelfe told Mr. *Brownes* fonne that his father had done that which he
deferved to die for, and were hee in any other place it would coft
him his life.   So fit for Government were thefe men, as to judge a
peaceable claime of right without any further difturbance or ftirre
made fhould thus deferve.   Neither indeed have wee further ftirred
then as before, ever refolving to reft in the determination of the
right honourable the Governour in chiefe and the reft of his honourable Affiftants of that Committee bee trufted with the affaires
of the Forraigne Englifh Plantations, affuring our felves what ever
might proceed either from mifinformation or want of due knowledge what was formerly done, would bee rectified upon the firft in-
formation and complaint made: Such were our thoughts of
them, and the juftice wee expected, and ftill hope to receive from
them.   And thus much for anfwer to that complaint.

In *pag.* 92. He layeth another groffe afperfion upon us, in faying,
There was diftance and alienation of affection betweene Plimouth *and
the* Maffachufets *at their firft comming, each thinking I am holier then
thou: and as if wee were now united on purpofe to fcatter them.* The world
knowes this to bee moft falfe.   Never people agreed better, maintaining both religious and civill Communion with each other, and
helping and being helpfull one to another upon all occafions: which
is fo well knowne, as if hee had not more then ordinary boldneffe
hee durft not affirme it.   Nor came the men of *Plimouth* from *Amfterdam* as hee reporteth but *Leyden,* a people that many of that
Church of *Amfterdam* would hardly allow communion withall:
but his pen is no flaunder, at leaft will not bee where this anfwer
fhall follow it.   And for his relation of the manner of the Indians
mourning for their Prince his death;   Truely had hee dyed a naturall death, 'tis their manner not onely fo to mourne for their
great *Sachims* which are Princes, but for ordinary men, women and
children as hee well knoweth or might know.

In *pag.* 93. He fnrther complaines of *Plimouth* and *Maffachufets* for
offering to goe out againft the *Nanohigganfets* to cut them off by the
fword.   And fo complaines alfo of Captaine *Standifh &c.   Anfw.*
I told you before how the Commiffioners for the United Colonies
meeting at *Hartford* by courfe, whofe meeting alwayes begins the
firft Thurfday in *Septemb.* fent for both the *Nanohigganfets* and
Uncus, who appeared, and a league agreed on: but the *Nanohig-*
                                                    ganfets

ganfets broke againe, and warred upon *Uncus* needlefly. The United Colonies admonifhed them againe and againe: and after no
admonition nor perfwafions would ferve, wee were then forced
to call the Commiffioners together at an extraordinary feafon on
purpofe, who finding it meet to take up Armes in the behalfe of
Vncus our Confederate,   whom by the agreement of the *Nanohig-*   Errata: l. 6,
ganfets fundry times , at divers meetings wee were bound , and   for whom, read
it was made lawfull to doe.   Hereupon the Commiffioners a-   which.]
greeing as before, fent out their Warrants to their feverall
and fpeciall Governments, and accordingly Forces were raifed
at a dayes warning.   But before this , in ftead of hearkening
to righteous Counfell, they threatened alfo the Englifh, faying,
they would make heapes of our dead bodies and cattle, as high
as their houfes , burne our habitations , make fpoile of our
goods, and ufed our Meffengers very difcurteoufly, &c.   And
for Captaine *Standifh*, this I heard him relate, that being at
the place of Rendezvouze, before the *Maffachufets* Forces came,
obferving that fome of the Inhabitants of *Providence* received
the *Indians* into their houfes familiarly, who had put themfelves
alfo into a pofture of Armes, and the place within a mile of *Secunck*
or *Rhehoboth* where Captaine *Standifh* lay; hee fent to *Providence*,
and required them to lay afide their neutrality, and either declare
themfelves on the one fide or other: For the warre being once
begun, hee would not beare with their carriage in entertaining,fur-
nifhing,and relieving the common enemy,but would difarm them,
&c. And whether neceffity put him not upon this courfe, or no,let
the Reader judge.
   And for the five hundred pound, 'tis true their hearts fayled to
fee *Plymouth* Forces appeare, and *Maffachuf.* both Horfe and Foot
upon their march on the one fide their Countrey,under Mr. *Edw.*
Gibbons who was chofen Generall of the United Colonies, with
the help of *Woofamequin*,whofe conftancy to *Plymouth* is welknown,
and *Pumham* and *Socononoco* with reference to *Maffachufets*with all
their men, attending the Englifh word of command.   And on the
other fide their Countrey the forces of *Coneetacut* and *Newhaven* ,
with all the ftrength of *Uncus*, waiting but for the word from the
Commiffioners to fall on.   Now I fay they were daunted efpecially
becaufe it came fo fuddenly upon them, wanting Mr. *Gorton* and his
friends who were not yet come; Hereupon they refolved to go to the
                                                            Com-

Commiffioners to *Maffachuf.* and compound, and did figne new
Articles to obferve the peace not onely with the United Colonies
but with *Uncus, Woofamequin, Pumham ,* and *Socononoco,* and o-
ther our Confederates, including all the Englifh in the land, to
make fatisfaction for wrongs to *Vncus ,* and to pay five hundred
pounds to the united Colonies,for the charge they put us to,which
indeed would not neare make it good, if they had paid it: but as
at other times, fo now, notwithftanding their Hoftages,they abufed
us grofly, firft fending falfe perfons; fecondly, breaking all other
their Covenants, and came at laft to a refolution , they would rather give the money (which is a Beade,as current as coin in all that
part of *America,* of their owne making) to the *Mowhakes* at once,to
cut us off,then to pay it according to Covenant.

And thus contrary to my refolution, I fee a neceffity of more
large anfwers then I intended; and indeed otherwife I fhould fpeak
riddles, and not fatisfie the Reader.   Although were it an Hiftory,
I have many remarkable paffages which here for brevity fake I muft
omit.   And if any think wee doe needlefly ingage in the troubles
betweene the *Indians?*   1. Let them know if wee fhould not here
and there keepe correfpondency with fome of them,"they would
foone joyne all together againft us.   2. The quarrall betweene
Uncus and *Nanohigganfet ,* arofe upon his cleaving to us: For the
great *Sachim Myantonimo* would have marryed *Uncus* daughter,and
fince *Peffachus* that fucceeded him would have marryed *Woofamequins* daughter, and all in policy to take them off from us; fo that indeed wee are neceffitated to it.   And 3. we are not out of hope in
time to bring them to the knowledge of Jefus Chrift , as will appeare by a fmall Treatife of that kinde.   But this one thing I defire
the Reader to take notice of, that when that great Prince *Myantonimo* hee fo much admires,had offered violence to *Woofamequin*(who
was under the protection of *Plymouth*) and miffing his perfon, returned onely with the plunder of his goods: Upon *Woofamequins*
complaint to *Plymouth,* that Government alone, it being before the
Union, fent Captain *Standifh* with a few men, not above 20. who
fent a meffage over the Bay of Salt water which parts *Woofamequin* from them, E*ither to make reftitution of his goods fo injurioufly
taken,or elfe to expect him to fetch them with a vengeance to their coft.* Hereupon they fent over every particular that could bee demanded, even
to a woodden difh, and falved up all againe; but this was before
                                                                    any

any malignant Englifh fate down fo neare them, and held counfell with them, before they had violated our perfons to them, reported us to bee bafe and low, out of favour with the King and State, &c. things very unworthy, abominable to be named,but that in defending the abufed Governments of the Country,I am forced to dang fuch ftrokes at thefe proud and turbulent enemies of the Countrey.

Next in *pag*. 94. that hee relateth of Mr. *Williams*; *viz*, the meſſengers taking him with them that were fent to the *Nanohigganfets*, in that troublefome time,*viz. being one caſt out of the Church*(Mr. *Cotton* fhould preach) *It was all one to take counfell of a witch, and that thofe that did it were worthy to die.* Upon which Mr. *Wilbour* one of the meffengers *was ready to die,*faith hee,*for feare hee fhould have been hanged.* This I cannot beleeve for thefe two Reafons: 1. Becaufe all men that know Mr. *Cotton*, know his moderation, wifdome and piety to bee fuch, as fuch an expreffion was not like to drop from him.   2. The ftricteft Government in *New-Engl.* that I know,takes no advantage in the law at a mans perfon for being excommunicated; infomuch as if he have an office, he holds it neverthelffe, and this,I know practifed, and therefore his relation unlike.   But that theMeffengers were directed to another for their interpreter I know, and that fome took offence at their practife I know alfo, but upon different grounds , which I forbeare to mention, being now to anfwer Mr.*Gorton*, and not Mr. *Williams*.

In *pag.* 93. which is the laſt *page* in his Booke that I fhall need to make anfwer to, and the thing hee there brings againft us is an anfwer to a doctrine one of their wives fhould heare delivered at *Maſſachufets* when fhee came to vifit them, from *Matth.* 24. 29. *and alluding to* Hebr. 12. 26, 27. briefly this doctrine there delivered, *fhould make the doctrine of the Apoſtles and the Churches in their times to bee but darkneffe. That the Miniſtery of the Apoſtles was and fhould be removed, &c.* which I defire the Reader to turne to; but bee affured through Gods mercy, by meanes of the late Bifhop of *Canterburies* perfecutions of the godly here, wee are fo excellently furnifhed with fhining Lights of the Gofpel, as no fuch blafphemous trafh as this could bee there delivered, and fo many able hearers, as if it fhould have been delivered by any, the Lord with-drawing his prefence from him, it would have been forthwith excepted againft and publifhed to the world.   But I am confident if fuch a thing were there heard, it was either from one of their owne com-

pany,

pany, or difciples made by them. And therefore I will paffe by
the anfwer alfo, as not concerning any difference between him and
us, and fo the reft of his writings to that end, and could wifh that
Narciffus-like hee were not fo much in love with his owne fhadow,
left it prove his ruine; there needing no other matter againft him
then his owne words and writings to render him odious to the
State here, as well as to *New-England* from whence he came.

AND now that I have finifhed what I conceive neceffary concerning Mr. *Gortons* fcandalous and flanderous Bookes, let me
briefly anfwer fome objections that I often meet withall againft the
Country of *New-England*. The firft that I meet with is, concerning the rife and foundation of our *New-England* Plantations; It
being alledged (though upon a great miftake by a late Writer) that
divifion or difagreement in the Church of *Leyden*, was the occafion, nay caufe of the firft Plantation in *New-England*; for faith the
Author, or to this effect, when they could no longer agree together,
the one part went to *New-England*, and began the Plantation at
Plymouth, which he makes the mother, as it were, of the reft of the
Churches, as if the foundation of our *New-England* Plantations
had been laid upon divifion or feparation, then which nothing is
moreuntrue: For I perfwade my felfe, never people upon earth
lived more lovingly together, and parted more fweetly then wee
the Church at *Leyden* did, not rafhly in a diftracted humour, but
upon joynt and ferious deliberation , often feeking the minde of
God by fafting and prayer, whofe gracious prefence we not onely
found with us, but his bleffing upon us from that time to this inftant, to the indignation of our adverfaries, the admiration of
ftrangers, and the exceeding confolation of our felves , to fee fuch
effects of our prayers and teares before our pilgrimage here bee ended.   And therefore briefly take notice of the true caufe of it.
   'Tis true, that that poor perfecuted flock of Chrift, by the malice
and power of the late Hierarchy were driven to *Leyden* in *Holland*,
there to beare witneffe in their practife to the Kingly Office of
Chrift Jefus in his Church: and there lived together ten yeares
under the United States, with much peace and liberty: But our
Reverend Paftor Mr. *John Robinfon* of late memory, and our grave
Elder Mr. *William Brewfter*, (now both at reft with the Lord) confidering

fidering amongft many other inconveniences, how hard the Country was where we lived, how many fpent their eftate in it, and were
forced to return for *England*; how grievous to live from under the
protection of the State of *England*; how like wee were to lofe our
language, and our name of Englifh; how little good wee did, or
were like to do to the Dutch in reforming the Sabbath; how una-
ble there to give fuch education to our children, as wee our felves
had received, &c.   They, I fay, out of their Chriftian care of the
flock of Chrift committed to them conceived , if Godwould bee
pleafed to difcover fome place unto us (though in *America*) and
give us fo much favour with the King and State of *England* , as to
have their protection there,where wee might enjoy the like liberty,
and where the Lord favouring our endeavours by his bleffing, wee
might exemplarily fhew our tender Country-men by our example
(no leffe burthened then our felves) where they might live, and
comfortably fubfift and enjoy the like liberties with us, being
freed from Antichriftian bondage , keep their names and Nation,
and not onely bee a meanes to enlarge the Dominions of our State,
but the Church of Chrift alfo , if the Lord have a people amongft
the Natives whither hee fhould bring us, &c.   Hereby in their
grave Wifdomes they thought wee might more glorifie God, doe
more good to our Countrey, better provide for our pofterity, and
live to be more refrefhed by our labours, then ever wee could doe in
Holland where we were.

Now thefe their private thoughts upon mature deliberation
they imparted to the Brethren of the Congregation, which after
much private difcuffion came to publike agitation, till at the length
the Lord was folemnly fought in the Congregation by fafting and
prayer to direct us, who moving our hearts more and more to the
worke, wee fent fome of good abilities over into *England* to fee
what favour or acceptance fuch a thing might finde with the King.
Thefe alfo found God going along with them, and got Sir *Edwin
Sands* a religious Gentleman then living, to ftirre in it, who procured Sir *Robert Nawnton* then principall Secretary of State to King
James of famous memory, to move his Majefty by a private motion to give way to fuch a people (who could not fo comfortably
live under the Government of another State) to enjoy their liberty
of Confcience under his gracious protection in *America*, where
they would endeavour the advancement of his Majefties Dominions,

ons, and the enlargement of the Goſpel by all due meanes.   This his Majeſty ſaid was a good and honeſt motion , and asking what profits might ariſe in the part wee intended (for our eye was upon the moſt Northern parts of *Virginia*) 'twas anſwered, Fiſhing.   To which hee replyed with his ordinary aſſeveration, *So God have my Soule 'tis an honeſt Trade , 'twas the Apoſtles owne calling , &c.* But afterwards he told Sir *Robert Nawnton,* (who took all occaſions to further it) that we ſhould confer with the Biſhops of *Canter. bury* and *London,* &c.   Whereupon wee were adviſed to perſiſt up- on his firſt approbation, and not to entangle our ſelves with them- which cauſed our Agents to repair to the *Virginia* Company,who in their Court demanded our ends of going; which being related , they ſaid the thing was of God, and granted a large Patent, and one of them lent us 300 *l. gratis* for three yeares,which was repaid.

Our Agents returning, wee further ſought the Lord by a pub- lique and ſolemn Faſt, for his gracious guidance.   And hereupon wee came to this reſolution, that it was beſt for one part of the Church to goe at firſt, and the other to ſtay, *viz.* the youngeſt and ſtrongeſt part to goe.   Secondly, they that went ſhould freely offer themſelves.   Thirdly, if the major part went, the Paſtor to goe with them; if not, the Elder onely.   Fourthly, if the Lord ſhould frowne upon our proceedings, then thoſe that went to returne, and the Brethren that remained ſtill there, to aſſiſt and bee helpfull to them, but if God ſhould bee pleaſed to favour them that went, then they alſo ſhould endeavour to helpe over ſuch as were poore and ancient,and willing to come; theſe things being agreed, the major part ſtayed, and the Paſtor with them for the preſent , but all in- tended (except a very few, who had rather wee would have ſtayed) to follow after.   The minor part, with Mr. *Brewſter* their Elder, reſolved to enter upon this great work(but take notice the difference of number was not great;)And when the Ship was ready to carry us away, the Brethren that ſtayed having againe ſolemnly ſought the Lord with us, and for us,and we further engaging our ſelves mutu- ally as before; they, I ſay, that ſtayed at *Leyden* feaſted us that were to goe at our Paſtors houſe being large, where wee refreſhed our ſelves after our teares, with ſinging of Pſalmes , making joyfull melody in our hearts, as well as with the voice, there being many of the Congregation very expert in Muſick; and indeed it was
the

the fweeteft melody that ever mine eares heard. After this they accompanyed us to *Delphs Haven*, where wee were to imbarque, and there feafted us againe; and after prayer performed by our Paftor, where a flood of teares was poured out, they accompanyed us to the Ship, but were not able to fpeake one to another for the abundance of forrow to part: but wee onely going aboard (the Ship lying to the Key) and ready to fet fayle, the winde being faire) wee gave them a volley of fmall fhot, and three peeces of Ordinance, and fo lifting up our hands to each other, and our hearts for each other to the Lord our God, we departed, and found his prefence with us in the midft of our manifold ftraits hee carryed us thorow. And if any doubt this relation, the *Dutch*, as I heare, at *Delphs*Haven preferve the memory of it to this day,and will inform them.

But falling with *Cape Cod* which is in *New-England*, and ftanding to the Southward for the place wee intended, wee met with many dangers, and the Mariners put back into the Harbour of the *Cape*, which was the 11. of *November*, 1620. where confidering Winter was come, the Seas dangerous, the feafon cold, the winds high, and being well furnifhed for a Plantation, we entered upon difcovery, and fetled at *Plymouth*, where God being pleafed to preferve and enable us, wee that went, were at a Thoufand pounds charge in fending for our Brethren that were behinde, and in providing there for them till they could reape a crop of their owne labours. And fo good Reader,I have given thee a true and faithfull account, though very briefe, of our proceedings,wherein thou feeft how a late Writer , and thofe that informed him, have wronged our enterprife.And truly what I have written, is far fhort of what it was,omitting for brevity fake many circumftances,as the large offers the *Dutch* offered us,either to have removed into *Zealand* and there lived with them: or if we would go on fuch adventures, to goe under them to *Hudfons* River (where they have fince a great plantation, &c.) and how they would freely have tranfported us, and furnifhed every family with cattle, &c. Alfo the Englifh Merchants thatjoyned with us in this expedition, whom wee fince bought out, which is fitter for an Hiftory, then an anfwer to fuch an Objection, (& I truft will be accomplifhed in good time.)By all which the Reader may fee there was no breach between us that went,and the brethren that ftayed,but fuch love as indeed isfeldome found on earth.   And

And for the many plantations that come over to us upon notice of Gods bleffing upon us, whereas 'tis falfly faid, they tooke *Pli-mouth* for their prefident as faft as they came. 'Tis true I confeffe that fome of the chiefe of them advifed with us (comming over to be freed from the burthenfome ceremonies then impofed in Eng-land) how they fhould doe to fall upon a right platforme of worfhip,and defired to that end fince God had honoured us to lay the foundation of a Common-weale,and to fettle a Church in it,to fhew them whereupon our practice was grounded; and if they found upon due fearch it was built upon the Word, they fhould be willing to take up what was ofGod. We accordingly fhewed them the Primitive practice for our warrant, taken out of the Acts of the Apoftles, and the Epiftles written to the feverall Churches by the faid Apoftles together with the Commandements of Chrift the Lord in the Gofpell, and other our warrants for every particular wee did from the booke of God. Which being by them well weigh-ed and confidered, they alfo entred into Covenant with God and one with another to walke in all his wayes revealed, or as they fhould bee made knowne unto them, and to worfhip him according to his will revealed in his written word onely, &c. So that here alfo thou maift fee they fet not the Church at *Plimouth* before them for example,but the Primitive Churches were and are their and our mutuall patterns and examples, which are onely worthy to be fol-lowed, having the bleffed Apoftles amongft them which were fent immediately by Chrift himfelfe and enabled and guided by the un-erring Spirit of God. And truly this is a patterne fit to bee fol-lowed of all that feare God, and no man or men to bee followed further then they follow Chrift and them.

Having thus briefly fhewed that the foundation of our *New-En-gland* Plantations was not laid upon Schifme, divifion, or Separati-on, but upon love, peace, and holineffe; yea, fuch love and mutuall care of the Church of *Leyden* for the fpreading of the Gofpel, the welfare of each other, and their pofterities to fucceeding generati-ons, as is feldome found on earth: And having fhewed alfo that the Primitive Churches are the onely pattern which the Churches of Chrift in *New-England* have in their eye, not following *Luther, Cal-vin, Knoxe, Ainfworth, Robinfon, Amies*, or any other, further then they follow Chrift and his Apoftles; I am earneftly requefted to cleare up another groffe miftake which caufed many, and ftill doth,

to

to judge the harder of *New-England*, and the Churches there, becaufe (fay they) *The Church of Plymouth which went firft from Leyden,
were Schifmaticks, Brownifts, rigid Separatifts, &c. having Mr.* Robinfon *for their Paftor, who made, and to the laft profeffed feparation from
other the Churches of Chrift,&c. And the reft of the Churches in New-
England holding communion with that Church, are to bee reputed fuch
as they are.*

For anfwer to this afperfion, Firft, he that knew Mr. *Robinfon*,
either by his Doctrine daily taught, or hath read his Apology publifhed not long before his death, or knew the practife of that Church
of Chrift under his government, or was acquainted with the wholfome counfell he gave that part of the Church which went for *New-
England* at their departure and afterward, might eafily refolve the
doubt, and take off the afperfion.

For his Doctrine, I living three yeares under his Miniftery, before
we began the worke of Plantation in *New-England* ; It was alwayes
againft feparation from any the Churches of Chrift, profeffing and
holding communion both with the *French* and *Dutch* Churches, yea,
tendering it to the *Scots* alfo, as I fhall make appeare more particularly anon. Ever holding forth how wary perfons ought to bee
in feparating from a Church, and that till Chrift the Lord departed
wholly from it, man ought not to leave it, onely to beare witneffe
againft the corruption that was in it. But if any object, he feparated from the Church of *England*, and wrote largely againft it; I acknowledge hee wrote largely againft it, but yet let me tell you, hee
allowed hearing the godly Minifters preach and pray in the publick
Affemblies; yea, hee allowed private communion not onely with
them, but all that were faithfull in Chrift Jefus in the Kingdome
and elfewhere upon all occafions; yea, honored them for the power
of godlineffe above all other the profeffors of Religion in the
world, nay, I may truly fay, his fpirit cleaved unto them, being fo
well acquainted with the integrity of their hearts, and care to walke
blameleffe in their lives, which was no fmall motive to him to perfwade us to remove from *Holland*, where wee might probably not
onely continue *Englifh*, but have and maintain fuch fweet communion with the godly of that Nation, as through Gods great mercy we
enjoy this day.

'Tis true, I confeffe he was more rigid in his courfe and way at
firft, then towards his latter end; for his ftudy was peace and union

fo far as might agree with faith and a good confcience;and for fchifm
and divifion,there was nothing in the world more hatefull to him:
But for the government of the Church of *England,* as it was in the
Epifcopall way,the Liturgy and ftinted prayers of the Church then;
yea, the conftitution of it as Nationall, and fo confequently the corrupt communion of the unworthy with the worthy receivers of the
Lords Supper, thefe things were never approved of him, but witneffed againft to his death,and are by the Church over which he was
to this day.   And if the Lord would be pleafed to ftir up the hearts
of thofe, in whom(under him) the power of Reformation lies, to
reform that abufe, that a diftinction might once be put between the
precious and the vile,particular Churches might be gathered by the
powerfull preaching of the Word, thofe onely admitted into communion, whofe hearts the Lord perfwades to fubmit unto the Iron
rod of the Gofpel; O how fweet then would the communion of the
Churches be! How thorow the Reformation! How eafie would
the differences be reconciled between the Presbyterian and Independent way! How would the God of peace which commandeth love
and good agreement fmile upon this Nation! How would the fubtle
underminers of it be difappointed, and the faithfull provoked to
fing fongs of praife and thankfgiving! Nay, how would the God
of order be glorified in fuch orderly walking of the Saints! And
as they have fought together for the liberties of the Kingdome, Ec-
clefiafticall and Civill; fo may they joyn together in the prefervation
of them (which otherwife, 'tis to be feared will not long continue)
and in the praifes of our God who hath been fo good to his poore
diftreffed ones, whom he hath delivered, and whom he will deliver
out of all their troubles. But I have made too great a digreffion,and
muft return.

In the next place I fhould fpeak of Mr. R*obinfons* Apology,where-
in he maketh a briefe defence againft many adverfaries, &c. But becaufe it is both in Latine and Englifh,of fmall price, and eafie to bee
had, I fhall forbeare to write of it, and onely refer the Reader to it,
for the differences between his congregation, and other the Reformed Churches.

The next thing I would have the Reader take notice of, is, that
however the church of *Leyden* differed in fome particulars, yet made
no Schifme or feparation from the Reformed Churches , but held
communion with them occafionally :For we ever placed a large difference

rence between thofe that grounded their practife upon the Word of God(tho differing from us in the expofition or underftanding of it) and thofe that hated fuch Reformers and Reformation, and went on in Antichriftian oppofition to it, and perfecution of it, as the late Lord Bifhops did, who would not in deed and truth(whatever their pretences were)that Chrift fhould rule over them. But as they often ftretched out their hands againft the faints; fo God hath withered the Arm of their power, thrown them down from their high & lofty feats, and flain the chiefe of their perfons, as well as the Hierarchy, that he might become an example to all thofe that rife againft God in his Sabbath, in the preaching of his Word, in his Saints,in the purity of his Ordinances. And I heartily defire that others may heare and feare withall.

As for the *Dutch*, it was ufuall for our Members that underftood the language,and lived in, or occafionally came over to *London*, to communicate with them, as one *John Jenny* a Brewer long did, his wife and family, &c. and without any offence to the Church: So alfo for any that had occafion to travell into any other part of the Netherlands they daily did the like: And our Paftor Mr.*Robinfon* in the time when Arminianifme prevailed fo much, at the requeft of the moft Orthodox Divines, as *Poliander, Feftus, Homlius, &c.* difputed daily againft *Epifcopius*(in the Academy at *Leyden*)and others the grand champions of that error,and had as good refpect amongft them, as any of their own Divines; Infomuch as when God took him away from them and us by death,the Univerfity, and Minifters of the City accompanied him to his grave with all their accuftomed folemnities; bewayling the great loffe that not onely that particular Church had, whereof he was Paftor; but fome of the chief of them fadly affirmed, that all the Churches of Chrift fuftained a loffe by the death of that worthy Inftrument of the Gofpel. I could inftance alfo divers of their members that underftood the Englifh tongue,and betook themfelves to the communion of our Church, went with us to *New*-England, as *Godbert Godbertfon, &c.* Yea,at this very inftant, another called *Mofes Symonfon*, becaufe a child of one that was in communion with the *Dutch* Church at *Leyden*, is admitted into Church-fellowfhip at *Plymouth* in *New*-England,and his children alfo to Baptifm,as wel as our own,and other *Dutch* alfo in communion at *Salem,&c.*

And for the *French* Churches that we held, and do hold communion

nion with them, take notice of our practife at *Leyden, viz.* that one *Samuel Terry* was received from the *French* Church there, into communion with us; alfo the wife of *Francis Cooke* being a *Walloone*, holds communion with the Church at *Plymouth*, as fhe came from the *French*,to this day, by vertue of communion of Churches; There is alfo one *Philip Delanoy* born of *French* parents, came to us from *Leyden* to *New-Plymouth*, who comming to age of difcerning, demanded alfo communion with us, & proving himfelf to be come of fuch parents as were in ful communion with the *French* Churches, was here upon admitted by the Church of P*lymouth*; and after upon his removal of habitation to *Duxburrow* where M.*Ralph Partridge* is Paftor of the Church; and upon Letters of recommendation from the Church at *Plymouth*, hee was alfo admitted into fellowfhip with the Church at *Duxburrow*, being fix miles diftant from *Plymouth*; and fo I dare fay,if his occafions lead him, may from Church to church throughout *New-England*.   For the truth is,the *Dutch* and *French* Churches either of them being a people diftinct from the world, and gathered into an holy communion, and not Nationall Churches, nay, fo far from it, as I verily beleeve the fixth perfon is not of the Church, the difference is fo fmall (if moderately pondered, between them and us)as we dare not for the world deny communion with them.

And for the Church of *Scotland*, however wee have had leaft occafion offered to hold communion with them; yet thus much I can and doe affirme, that a godly Divine comming over to *Leyden* in *Holland*, where a Booke was printed, *Anno* 1619. as I take it, fhewing the nullity of *Perth* Affembled, whom we judged to bee the Author of it, and hidden in *Holland* for a feafon to avoid the rage of thofe evill times (whofe name I have forgotten;)   This man being very converfant with our Paftor Mr. *Robinfon*, and ufing to come to hear him on the Sabbath, after Sermon ended, the Church being to partake in the Lords Supper, this Minifter ftood up and defired hee might, without offence, ftav and fee the manner of his adminiftration, and our participation in that Ordinance; To which our Paftor anfwered in thefe very words, or to this effect, *Reverend Sir, you may not onely ftay to behold us, but partake with us, if you pleafe, for wee acknowledge the Churches of Scotland to be the Churches of Chrift,&c.* The Minifter alfo replyed to this purpofe, if not alfo in the fame words; *That for his part hee could comfortably partake with the Church, and willingly would, but that it is poffible fome of his brethren of Scotland might*

might take offence at his act; which he defired to avoid in regard of the opinion the Englifh Churches which they held communion withall had of us: However he rendered thanks to Mr. *Robinfon*, and defired in that refpect to be onely a fpectator of us. Thefe things I was earneftly requefted to publifh to the world by fome of the godly Presbyterian party, who apprehend the world to bee ignorant of our proceedings, conceiving in charity that if they had been knowne, fome lateWriters and Preachers would never have written and fpoke of us as they did, and ftill doe as they have occafion: But what they ignorantly judge, write, or fpeak of us, I truft the Lord in mercy wil paffe by.

In the next place, for the wholfome counfell Mr. *Robinfon* gave that part of the Church whereof he was Paftor, at their departure from him to begin the great worke of Plantation in *New-England*, amongft other wholfome Inftructions and Exhortations, hee ufed thefe expreffions, or to the fame purpofe; We are now ere long to part afunder, and the Lord knoweth whether ever he fhould live to fee our faces again: but whether the Lord had appointed it or not, he charged us before God and his bleffed Angels, to follow him no further then he followed Chrift. And if God fhould reveal any thing to us by any other inftrument of his, to be as ready to receive it, as ever we were to receive any truth by his Miniftery: For he was very confident the Lord had more truth and light yet to breake forth out of his holy Word. He took occafion alfo miferably to bewaile the ftate and condition of the Reformed Churches, who were come to a period in Religion, and would goe no further then the inftruments of their Reformation: As for example, the *Lutherans* they could not be drawne to goe beyond what *Luther* faw, for whatever part of Gods will he had further imparted and revealed to *Calvin*, they will rather die then embrace it. And fo alfo, faith he, you fee the *Calvinifts*, they ftick where he left them: A mifery much to bee lamented; For though they were precious fhining lights in their time, yet God had not revealed his whole will to them: And were they now living, faith hee, they would bee as ready and willing to embrace further light, as that they had received. Here alfo he put us in mind of our Church-Covenant (at leaft that part of it) whereby wee promife and covenant with God and one with another, to receive whatfoever light or truth fhall be made known to us from his written Word: but withall exhorted us to take heed what

we

we received for truth, and well to examine and compare, and weigh it with other Scriptures of truth, before we received it; For, faith he, *It is not poffible the Chriftian world fhould come fo lately out of fuch thick Antichriftian darkneffe, and that full perfeftion of knowledge fhould breake forth at once.*

Another thing hee commended to us, was, that wee fhould ufe all meanes to avoid and fhake off the name of *Brownift*, being a meer nick-name and brand to make Religion odious, and the profeffors of it to the Chriftian world; and to that end, faid hee, I fhould be glad if fome godly Minifter would goe over with you, or come to you, before my comming; For, faid hee, there will bee no difference between the uncomformable Minifters and you , when they come to the practife of the Ordinances out of the Kingdome: And fo advifed us by all meanes to endeavour to clofe with the godly party of the Kingdome of *England,*and rather to ftudy union then divifion; *viz.* how neare we might poffibly, without fin clofe with them, then in the leaft meafure to affect divifion or feparation from them. And be not loath to take another Paftor or Teacher, faith hee, for that flock that hath two fhepheards is not indangered, but fecured by it. Many other things there were of great and weighty confequence which he commended to us, but thefe things I thought good to relate, at the requeft of fome well-willers to the peace and good agreement of the godly, (fo diftracted at prefent about the fettling of Church-government in the Kingdom of *England*) that fo both fides may truly fee what this poor defpifed Church of Chrift now at *New-Plymouth* in *New-England,*but formerly at *Leyden* in *Holland,* was and is; how far they were and ftill are from feparation from the Churches of *Chrift*, efpecially thofe that are Reformed.

'Tis true, we profeffe and defire to practife a feparation from the world,& the works of the world, which are works of the flefh, fuch as the Apoftle fpeaketh of, *Ephef.*5.19,20,21. 1 *Cor.*6.9,10,11. and *Ephef.*2. 11,12. And as the Churches of Chrift are all Saints by calling, fo we defire to fee the grace of God fhining forth, (at leaft feemingly, leaving fecret things to God)in all we admit into church fellowfhip with us, & to keep off fuch as openly wallow in the mire of their fins, that neither the holy things of God, nor the communion of the Saints may be leavened or polluted thereby. And if any joyning to us formerly,either when we lived at *Leyden* in *Holland,*or fince we came to *New-England,* have with the manifeftation of their
faith

faith and profeffion of holineffe held forth therewith feparation from the Church of *England*, I have divers times, both in the one place, and the other, heard either *Mr. Robinfon* our Paftor, or *Mr. Brewfter* our Elder ftop them forthwith, fhewing them that wee required no fuch things at their hands, but only to hold forth faith in Chrift Jefus, holineffe in the feare of God , and fubmiffion to every Ordinance and appointment of God , leaving the Church of *England* to themfelves, and to the Lord before whom they fhould ftand or fall, and to whom wee ought to pray to reforme what was amiffe amongft them. Now this Reformation we have lived to fee performed and brought about by the mighty power of God, this day in a good meafure , and I hope the Lord Jefus will perfeƈt his work of Reformation, till all be according to the good pleafure of his will. By all which I defire the Reader to take notice of our former and prefent praƈtife notwithftanding all the injurious and fcandalous taunting reports are paffed on us. And if thefe things will not fatisfie , but wee muft ftill fuffer reproach, and others for our fakes , becaufe they and wee thus walke , our praƈtife being for ought wee know, wholly grounded on the written Word , without any addition or humane invention knowne to us , taking our patterne from the Primitive Churches , as they were regulated by the bleffed Apoftles in their owne dayes, who were taught and inftruƈted by the Lord Jefus Chrift, and had the unerring and all-knowing Spirit of God to bring to their remembrance the things they had heard: I fay, if wee muft ftill fuffer fuch reproach, notwithftanding our charity towards them who will not be in charity with us; Gods will be done.

The next afperfion caft upon us, is, that we will not fuffer any that differ from us never fo little to refide or cohabite with us; no not the Presbyterian Government which differeth fo little from us. To which I anfwer, our praƈtife witneffeth the contrary. For 'tis well knowne that Mr. *Parker* and Mr. *Noyce* who are Minifters of the Church at *Newberry* are in that way and fo knowne fo farre as a fingle Congregation can bee exercifed in it ; yet never had the leaft moleftation or difturbance, and have and finde as good refpeƈt from Magiftrates and people as other Elders in the Congregationall or Primitive way. 'Tis knowne alfo that Mr. *Hubbard* the Minifter at *Hengam* hath declared himfelfe for that way: nay which is more then ever I heard of the other two, hee refufeth to
baptize

baptzie no children that are tendred to him (although this liberty ftands not upon a Presbyterian bottome) and yet the Civill State never molefted him for it: onely comming to a Synod held in the Country the laft yeare, which the Magiftrates called, requefting the Churches to fend their Elders and fuch other as might bee able to hold forth the light of God from his written word in cafe of fome doubts which did arife in the Country: I fay hee comming the laft fitting of the Affembly which was adjourned to the eighth of *June* next, was in all meekneffe and love requefted to bee prefent and hold forth his light hee went by in baptizing all that were brought to him, hereby waving the practife of the Churches, which he promifing to take into confideration they refted in his anfwer. So alfo 'tis wel known, that before thefe unhappy troubles arofe in *England* and *Scotland*, there were divers Gentlemen of *Scotland* that groaned under the heavy preffaries of thofe times, wrote to *New-England* to know whether they might freely be fuffered to exercife their Prefbyteriall government amongft us.   And it was anfwered affirmatively they might: and they fending over a Gentleman to take a view of fome fit place; A River called *Meromeck* neare *Ipfwich* and *Newberry* aforefaid, was fhewed their Agent, which he well liked, and where wee have fince four townes fettled, and more may bee for ought I know, fo that there they might have had a compleate Presbytery and whither they intended to have come: but meeting with manifold croffes being halfe Seas thorow they gave over their intendments, and as I have heard thefe were many of the Gentlemen that firft fell upon the late Covenant in *Scotland*: by all which will eafily appeare how wee are here wronged by many; and the harder meafure as wee heare impofed upon our brethren for our fakes, nay pretending our example for their prefident. And laft of all, not long before I came away certaine difcontented perfons in open Court of the *Maffachufets*, demanding that liberty, it was freely and as openly tendred to them; fhewing their former practices by mee mentioned: but willed not to expect that wee fhould provide them Minifters &c. for the fame, but getting fuch themfelves they might exercife the Presbyterian Government at their libertie, walking peaceably towards us as wee trufted we fhould doe towards them.   So that if our brethren here fhall bee reftrained they walking peaceably, the example muft not be taken from us, but arife from fome other principle.

But

But it will not bee objected though you deale thus with the Pref-byterian way, yet you have a fevere law againft Anabaptifts, yea one was whipt at *Maffachufets* for his Religion? and your law banifh-eth them? *Anfw.* 'Tis true, the *Maffachufets* Governement have fuch a law as to banifh, but not to whip in that kinde. And certaine men defiring fome mitigation of it; It was anfwered in my hear-ing. 'Tis true, we have a fevere law, but wee never did or will exe-cute the rigour of it upon any, and have men living amongft us, nay fome in our Churches of that judgement, and as long as they carry themfelves peaceably as hitherto they doe, wee will leave them to God, our felves having performed the duty of brethren to them. And whereas there was one whipt amongft us; 'tis true wee knew his judgement what it was: but had hee not carried himfelfe fo con-temptuoufly towards the Authority God hath betrufted us with in an high exemplary meafure, wee had never fo cenfured him: and therefore he may thank himfelf who fuffered as an evill doer in that refpect. But the reafon wherefore wee are loath either to repeale or alter the law, is, Becaufe wee would have it remaine in force to beare witneffe againft their judgement and practife which we con-ceive them to bee erroneous.

And yet nevertheleffe faid the Governour to thofe preferred the requeft, you may tel our friends in *England,* whither yee arefome of you going, fince the motion proceedeth from fuch as wee know move it in love to us, wee will ferioufly take it into confideration at our next Generall Court. So that thou maift perceive good Rea-der that the worft is fpoken of things in that kinde.

Furthermore in the Government of *Plimouth,* to our great griefe, not onely the Paftor of a Congregation waveth the adminiftration of baptifme to Infants, but divers of his Congregation are fallen with him, and yet all the meanes the civill power hath taken againft him and them, is to ftirre up our Elders to give meeting and fee if by godly conference they may bee able to convince and reclaime him, as in mercy once before they had done by Gods bleffing upon their labours. Onely at the forefaid Synod, two were ordered to writeto him in the name of the Affembly, and to requeft his prefence at their next meeting aforefaid to hold forth his light hee goeth by in waving the practife of the Churches; with promife if it be light, to walke by it: but if it appeare otherwife, then they truft hee will returne againe to the unity of practice with them. And for the o-
ther

CARL A. RUDISILL LIBRARY
LENOIR RHYNE COLLEGE

ther two Governments of *Coneetacut* and *Newhaven*, if either have any law in force againft them , or fo much as need of a law in that kinde, 'tis more then I have heard on.

For our parts(I mean the Churches of *New-Engl.*) we are confident through Gods mercy, theway of God in which we walke,and according to which wee perform our Worfhip and fervice to Him, concurreth with thofe Rules our bleffed Saviour hath left upon record by the Evangelifts and Apoftles, and is agreeable with the practife of thofe Primitive Churches mentioned in the *Acts*, and regulated by the fame Apoftles, as appeareth not onely in that Evangelicall Hiftory, but in their Epiftles to the feverall Churches there mentioned; yet neverthelesse if any thorow tenderneffe of Confcience be otherwife minded, to fuch wee never turn a deafe eare, nor become rigorous, though we have the ftreame of Authority on our fides. Nay, if in the ufe of all means we cannot reclaim them,knowing the *wifdome that is from above is firft pure, then peaceable, gentle,eafie to be intreated, full of mercy and good fruits,without partiality,and without hypocrifie,and the fruit of righteoufneffe is fowne in peace,of them that make peace,* according to *James* 3.17,18. And if any differing from us bee anfwerable to this Rule in their lives and converfations, we do not exercife the Civill fword againft them. But for fuch as *Gorton* and his company, whofe wifdome feems not to be from above,as appeareth in that it is *full of envying, ftrife, confufion,* Jam. 3.15, 16. being therein fuch as the Apoftle *Jude* fpeaks on, *v.* 8. viz. *earthly, fenfuall, devillifh*; who *v.*16. *defpife dominion, and fpeak evill of dignities.* Thefe *v.*12,13.are *murmurers, complayners, walkers after their own lufts, and their mouth fpeaketh great fwelling words,* being *clouds without water, carried about of winds, trees whofe fruit withereth, without fruit, twice dead, plucked up by the roots, raging waves of the fea, foaming out their owne fhame, wandring ftarres, to whom* (without repentance, which I much defire to fee, or hear of in him, if it may ftand with the will of God) *is referved the blackneffe of darkneffe for ever.* Thefe I fay are to be proceeded with by another rule,and not to bee borne: who fuffer as evil doers, and are a fhame to Religion which they profeffe in word,but deny in their lives and converfations. Thefe every tender confcience abhors,and will juftifie and affift the *higher Powers God hath ordained,* againft fuch carnall Gofpellers, *who beare not the fword in vaine,* Rom. 13.but execute Gods vengeance on fuch: for the Civill Magiftrate is *the Minifter of God, a Revenger to execute wrath on him that doth evil.* And

there-

therefore a broad difference is to be put between fuch evill doers, and thofe tender confciences who follow the light of Gods Word in their owne perfwafions, (though judged erroneous by the places where they live) fo long as their walking is anfwerable to the rules of the Gofpel, by preferving peace, and holding forth holineffe in their converfations amongft men.

Thus much I thought good to fignifie, becaufe we of *New-England* are faid to be fo often propounded for an example. And if any will take us for a prefident, I defire they may really know what wee doe, rather then what others ignorantly or malitioufly report of us, affuring my felf that none will ever be lofers by following us fo far as we follow Chrift: Which that we may doe, and our pofterities after us, the Father of our Lord Jefus Chrift, & our Father, accept in Chrift what is according to him, difcover, pardon, and reform what is amiffe amongft us; and guide us and them by the affiftance of the holy Ghoft for time to come, till time fhal be no more; that the Lord our God may ftill delight to dwell amongft his Plantations and Churches there by his gracious prefence, and may goe on bleffing to bleffe them with heavenly bleffings in thefe earthly places, that fo by his bleffing they may not onely grow up to a Nation, but become exemplary for good unto others. And let all that wifh wel to *Sion* fay *Amen.*

FINIS.

ERRATA.

In the title of p. 9, &c. to 37. in ftead, of the Magiftrates of *Bofton* in *New-Engl.* r. *of Maffachufets in New England*; p 11. l. 27. for purpofe God, r. *purpofe of God*; p. 14. for day of, r. *day of the*; p. 30 l. 17. for Cope, r. *cup*; alfo l. 18 for cope, r. *cup*; alfo l. 21. for Judas, r. *as Judas*; p. 32. l. 3. leave out *to*; p. 54. l. 10. for by, r. *in*; p. 67. l. 37. for complaining, r. *complained*; p. 79. l. 26. for with as indeed, r. *with them as*; p. 83. l.23. for and, put (p. 85. l. 6. for whom, r. *which.*